Finding Your Cape

Mare McHale

Alice,
you do you
♥ mare
oxox

[signature]

Finding Your Cape

◆◆◆

**How to course-correct and achieve greatness
when things don't go as planned**

◆◆◆

Mare McHale

Table of Contents

For Thomas,

May you always feel your cape behind you.

PRE-FLIGHT

Chapter 1:

Spoiler Alert

THREE DAYS INTO my new life, I asked my friend a question that exposed how overwhelmed I was.

"I just don't know how to do this: how am I supposed to plan his funeral?"

It had been three days since I'd seen him. Three days of intense, numbing, black-out grief. Three days with a label I did not choose: widow.

A widow, alone at the age of 33, after her husband took his own life.

A widow, raising a special needs son by herself.

A widow, who knew all too well what it was like to lose a father at a young age.

A widow left to somehow create a new "normal," whatever that might be.

My friend repeated one thing to me on the phone that day and for months afterwards: *You can do anything for ten minutes.*

I dully listened to her voice on the phone from thousands of kilometres away. It was as if I was hearing the words in an out-of-body experience. Like I was floating above, watching the scene unfold without feeling like it could be real.

You can do anything for ten minutes. Then you focus on the next ten minutes. Then the next.

I somehow got myself to the funeral home that day to make the endless decisions to lay my husband Jeremy to rest. It feels impossible to plan a funeral for a 35-year-old. It is surreal being led to a room filled with urns and headstone mock-ups, told to pick one out for your husband, who just a week ago was happily watching a parade with his son, texting funny photos of the two of them eating food, laying in the grass, and staring at the sky.

But you can do anything for ten minutes.

I can't even guess how many times I have had to take things ten minutes at a time.

Spoiler alert: my story does have a happy ending with joy and love and peace. In fact, it has a happy middle and end. I've been sharing my story for the past few years on the radio, online, in my videos, and in masterclass sessions, with the hopes that people will feel less alone. That's why I created the Mareathoner community—a tight-knit online group of like-minded people who are trying to better themselves while being kind, supportive, and understanding of others, in addition to honouring themselves. We don't give up, we know who we are, we lift others up despite our own struggles and we celebrate each other's successes. We support one another; we love and are loved. The Mareathoners have been through shit, but we don't act like shit.

The details are different, but anyone can see themselves in my story. We've all suffered loss, disappointment, pain, life-shifts, incredible hardship, and more. But what do we do when faced with unimaginable circumstances? That's what interests me. That's what propels me to share. That's what pushed me to write this book.

That's also what has prompted me to share something, inspired by my dad, that has been my saving grace in good times and bad. It's more than a lucky penny or quotable meme—it's a state of mind. There can be so many days that we have to take the Mareathon 10 minutes at a time. Like when my father suddenly passed away. Like when my husband was found by police, hours after his death. Like times in my youth when I made some less-than-stellar choices. Like when my child was diagnosed, on two occasions, with life-altering special needs. Even though I have been publicly sharing my story for years, I have never shared this secret. My secret weapon, if you will.

I have a cape.

My cape's secret strength is with me every day, in the worst and best of times. I call it to attention at a moment's notice and it's right there, waiting. I had the strength to claw my way out of the utmost darkness of despair, heartache, and loss, to an empowered place of love and peace because the cape helped me tap a reservoir of superhero strength already inside me—even when I didn't believe it was there.

And guess what: it's also inside you. It's in every single one of us, waiting.

Baby, you're about to discover your own cape.

Ready? Let's fly.

Chapter 2:

Prepare to Propel

WE'VE ALL BEEN there: Your palms are sweaty. Your breath is tight and shallow. Your stomach is turning over and over, flipping in knots. You are about to head into a situation you've been dreading, but the moment of truth is finally here. There's no backing out now. Maybe it's a meeting with your child's teacher, or your boss, or your girlfriend. You step out of your car, knees weak, hand shaking as you close the door on the little sanctuary of the car behind you. Thud. The door closes; there's no turning back. You're now worried the person you're meeting can see you through their window, so you straighten up and try to pretend as if it's just an ordinary day. The blood pounds in your ears, threatening to give you away, as you make your way into the unknown.

Total panic, right? I feel jittery just writing this! That scenario used to see me making any excuse to drive away and avoid confrontation, totally ignoring the issue at hand.

Anxiety. Panic. Stress.

Now, imagine that same scenario with a twist. You have a voice in your head, whispering encouragement, boosting your fortitude, reminding you to breathe, cheering that you're good enough, saying that you've got this, and indicating when it's okay to leave. Your own hype squad if you will, ready at a moment's notice.

Wouldn't that be brilliant?!

Well, in this book I am going to give you the tools to bring out your already existing cape. Something with you at a moment's notice, pulled from your very own psyche. It's there, but it may be dusty, waiting in the wings patiently for you to turn towards it.

You're going to discover your own kick-ass secret weapon: a superhero's cape.

This cape, as you will learn, doesn't have to look like a typical superhero's cape. You can envision it however you like. It could be a sassy, high-end cape, one that would cost more in a luxury boutique than the downpayment on my house. (Sometimes when I am wearing a long cardigan, I feel powerful as it flaps in the breeze while I strut down the street.) Or you could envision it to mimic a hero's cape, bravely waving in the wind.

My hope for you as you read this book is that you too feel your cape start to take shape. Mine gently attaches near my collar bone, drawing my shoulders back, chin lifted, eyes forward.

The possibilities of what your own cape can help you achieve are limitless. For example:

★ increase focus and productivity
★ be more present
★ stand up for yourself
★ walk away from a toxic relationship
★ sit with someone in pain without taking on their pain yourself
★ be patient with your children, your spouse and even yourself
★ let the opinions of others slide right off of your cape

★ take time to discover what you want to do, not what has always been expected of you
★ enjoy the moment
★ find pleasure in the simplest things
★ reinvent yourself

The cape is part mindset and part action. I mean, you need to move forward in order to get that cape rippling in the wind, right?

Finding Your Cape:

It's time for you to start building your own cape. To do this, pull out a notebook and pen. There will be prompts throughout this book; in order to really define your own cape and start using your own secret weapon, you'll need to write things down.

Organizational Psychologist Dr. Benjamin Hardy says, "as you read and re-write your goals daily, they'll become forged into your subconscious mind. Eventually, your dreams and vision will consume your inner world and quickly become your physical reality."

Start with a brain dump. This is the term I use to describe a free-writing exercise. Start imagining your own cape and describe it. What does it look like? Does it have colour? More than one colour? What images are woven within its fabric? You could name your cape. You can imagine its size and shape and what it looks like as you walk.

Just write. There is no judgement in a journal and the cape only shows love and support. Write as much as you can until you start to really feel the cape rise up. We will write more about your cape. My friend, this is just the beginning.

Chapter 3:

My Dad—The Inventor of the Flying Cape

MY DAD MADE Superman fly. No, really.

Let me backup a bit: my dad's hobby was building and flying model airplanes. I'm talking massive, six-foot wingspan planes that he flew all over North America. My dad is even in the Model Airplane Association of Canada (MAAC) Hall of Fame. He always wanted to build and fly something that was unique. Instead of creating common planes, he would choose very specific types and models, like the DeHavilland Tiger Moth or the Sorrell Hiperbipe, which currently hangs in my home. He was always working in our basement, with the radio or television on for background noise, as he was tinkering on the next model. When I was really little, my dad made a doghouse with Snoopy from the Peanuts cartoon sitting on top. It even flew! It was always something with him. My dad loved to create and take things to the next level, even to the point of deciding to build a flying man! I asked my brother, Sean, how our dad came up with the idea of building a life-sized, flying, Superman. Sean said our dad loved finding something really challenging to make. Plus, as a teacher, he knew that if he created something unique, it would inspire others and promote the hobby he loved so much.

The model was completely created from scratch. He decided to go with Superman because he believed it was important that the character be instantly recognizable, and my dad envisioned the cape acting like the wing. The first model was made almost entirely out of blue insulation foam. It had built-in controls for roll and pitch, as well as a rudder on the top of the cape. It was hand-launched, requiring someone to give it a good running start. My brother said it needed someone who was athletic to give it a chance to launch, as it was under-powered and non-aerodynamic. It only had about a 50/50 chance of taking off. Those odds are probably being generous. Superman didn't have landing gear (this would detract from the illusion of him being a flying person, of course), so he would land on his belly.

Superman was always a crowd-favourite. We went to a lot of flying meets during my childhood and I can remember grown men excitedly running up to my dad, asking if Superman would be flying that day. The crowd would hold its collective breath to see if the Man of Steel would, in fact, gain altitude. Sean and I both remember a meet when Superman had a bumpy landing, and his head came off and rolled down the runway! My dad raced to repair Superman and fly him a second time that day. His efforts were met with a collective sigh of relief among parents and kids alike, and this time his head remained firmly on his shoulders!

As the lore of the Man with the Flying Superman grew, my dad, ever the problem-solver, created a second model. This time Superman's cape was replaced with a lighter material, incorporating an airfoil shape to provide better lift and a more powerful motor. He also built a secret trap door in the belly which allowed the person hand-launching to get a better grip and stronger throw.

My dad loved flying Superman. Neither versions of Superman were aerodynamic, which made them difficult to fly. Even though it was never easy, the result was always worth the effort.

Isn't that a metaphor for life? The things that yield the most rewarding results are never easy, or smooth. We want to be as aerodynamic as possible while navigating life, with little dragging us down.

Unfortunately, there were a limited number of times my dad made Superman fly. I was just 19 when he passed away. These memories seem like a long time ago, but they are filled with strong emotions. I remember his joy. I remember his excitement of bringing it down to the school field, and setting it up for lift-off. The expression on his face when it steadied and flew. Honestly, I don't think he was doing it for his own satisfaction or joy. He loved to see a look of wonder and amazement in a sea of faces. My dad wanted to make someone else's day a little brighter. He was always the first to lighten the mood, jump up to help or ease another person's load. Those are the character benchmarks I strive for in my own life.

But life isn't perfect, is it? The ups are matched by the downs. We're flying high one moment, and then sometimes we crash down the next. Trust me, I know. Plenty of crash landings in my world, and I bet you are imagining your own. We all have them. My dad's death shook our family, leaving all of us unsure of how we'd find direction without the gentle giant who sat at the head of the table. My sister and I decided to honour his memory with matching Superman tattoos.

(Want some 'do-as-I-say-not-as-I-do' advice? Never get a back massage the morning of a back tattoo. I thought it was genius: I would be so relaxed that it wouldn't even hurt. Wrong! My muscles were so tender that I winced and squirmed through the entire thing while my sister breezed through it. We also got it done in someone's basement which I know doesn't sound smart... okay, it definitely wasn't. Please only get tattooed in a reputable shop.) The symbol makes it feel as though he's always with me. Even though I giggle at people's disappointment when I can't share their love of Clark Kent, I do savour every opportunity to regale them with tales of my dad and his life-sized flying Superman.

As we neared the one-year anniversary of his passing, a legitimate firestorm was destroying the mountainside in the valley where we lived. Started by a single lightning strike during one of the driest summers on record, the fire tore through more than tens of thousands of hectares of land, forcing 27,000 people to evacuate their homes. They frantically packed what they could at a moment's notice and barreled down the streets, not knowing what they'd return to, if anything at all. Some escaped while hot embers threatened to burn their vehicles, the fire jumping to roads in front of them. It was like something out of a blockbuster movie, but it was happening 45 minutes away from our house. One evening a friend and I drove to a lookout at the water's edge and sat in my car, watching the uncontrollable fire ravage the mountainside. It was late at night, but the radio station we tuned into had live announcers working around the clock to share updates. I distinctly remember listening as terrified residents called in to ask what streets were evacuated. The announcers frantically rifled through pages of information, repeating the names of streets over and over again, adding new ones constantly. I can still hear the panic in callers' voices as the announcers listed their street and added, "You need to drop everything and leave now. The fire is coming fast and hot and there is no time. Get off the phone and get in your car. Be safe." This went on for hours, call after call. These radio announcers saved lives. All told, 239 buildings burned down in a matter of weeks. That was a defining moment in my life. I felt the cape. It was in that moment that I understood the value of public radio and helping others in crisis. In an instant, I knew radio was my calling and, more specifically, my purpose would be to help my community. That was the exact day I realized that, in helping others, I would help heal myself.

It dawned on me: just like my dad, I could be my own hero. My dad always listened to the radio and as a family we would gather in front of the TV to watch the six o'clock news. Everything had been leading to this. Three weeks later, I started journalism school and was quickly on my way. I don't remember feeling anything but determined to start my career in journalism. In fact, before the first month of school was up, I sat in my professor's office, asking for the most direct route to a job in radio. My cape carried me. I continued to replay those phone calls into the radio station during the fire over and over in my head. The cape reminded me of my mission to help others and secure a career.

Here's a fun fact: the cape is always there. It's always with me. It's always with you. It's not stashed in a box somewhere, needing to be dry-cleaned. You don't need to coax it out of hiding. It's there at a moment's notice, ready to report for duty.

Your cape is patiently waiting for you to discover its power and realize it's been there all along, waiting to spring into action. It matches every outfit and is perfect for every occasion.

The cape will honour all of your feelings. It doesn't judge or hold a grudge, it builds on everything you're feeling. It protects you from attack, helps you take deeper breaths and builds you up. It wants you to feel the feels and use those feelings and emotions to fuel its strength. Every experience or emotion is woven into its tapestry, building with one experience and the next. It reminds you of where you've been and gives you clarity on where you're going. Your story fuels the cape and powers your courage. Some tears will weave into the fibres of your cape and the rest will gently flow off the cape, as you let them go.

Your cape also holds dear the achievements you've accomplished—big or small. I picture the milestones as the thread that darns a hole or sews a seam. I remember my mum or my nana sitting at their sewing machines, creating garments seemingly out of thin air. With just a small strand of thread, they sewed different fabrics together to create something beautiful. I see those threads of accomplishments stitching strength into your cape. They piece together the tapestry of your life. Things like graduating college, leaving that no-good boyfriend, and buying your first house. Things like putting together that bed frame alone, learning how to make the perfect quinoa, and finding the time to meditate. Every time you keep a promise to yourself, especially when no one is looking, you weave perseverance into that cape.

The cape gains lift from health, community, love, action, patience, vulnerability, courage, joy, history, and confidence—just to name a few.

What about people who do bad things—do they have a cape? Yes, but it doesn't serve them. The cape is weakened by toxic behaviour. That cape is ready and waiting to support a person when they are prepared to take the smart, healthy path back to right their wrongs. Hurt people hurt people, and the cape wants nothing to do with that until the person recognizes a need for change and owns up to their behaviour. At the end of the day, the cape is for the superhero—not the villain.

Is everyone a superhero? Do we all have superpowers but just don't know it? The name sounds hella daunting. But, yeah, we are all superheroes. Think of all the stuff you have done to get where you are today, all the ways you've developed, all the blood your heart has diligently pumped, all the breaths you have taken without even realizing it. Heck, just think of everything that's gone into getting you through today alone. We are pure magic, baby.

To boost your power, you must do the work that will increase your ability to fly. Your aerodynamics. No superhero is great solely on their own, and neither are we. My dad realized that even superheroes needed some extra power in order to fly.

Chapter 4

Mareathoners

I 'M A HUGGER AND when someone says, "I'm a Mareathoner," then a big squeeze is definitely in order! I love it
when people come up to me and reveal themselves. (Not
in that way, you perv.) It's hilarious when a guy admits he's a
Mareathoner. This is how it usually goes: "My wife watches
your videos all the time. She watches them in bed. So Mare,
it's like we are in bed together, haha. She's allllways watching
you and I just didn't get it. But, uh, actually... thanks. I love
what you do and some of the videos have really helped me.
Think the official Mareathoner arrow hat will fit me too?"

I am infinitely grateful for this community. It's a safe
space where no one is judgmental and everyone is working to
better themselves, even in the most minuscule way. In a study
done by Harvard Medical School, which examined data from
more than 309,000 people, it was found that "lack of strong
relationships increased the risk of premature death from all
causes by 50%—an effect on mortality risk roughly compara-
ble to smoking up to 15 cigarettes a day, and greater than
obesity and physical inactivity." Building a community or
tribe is important, and even life-saving!

Later in the book, I will tell you the story of how this Mareathoner community was formed, but right now I want to dedicate a chapter to this group, which is unlike any other I know.

What does it mean to be a Mareathoner? We listen, we accept, we challenge, we support, we grow, we laugh, we love, we cry, and we hold each other up.

We've been through shit, but we don't act like shit.

This is a Safe Space: Mareathoners are forever thanking me for creating the community, saying it's their favourite place on the internet. Well, it's mine too. I may run the group, but it gives me such fulfilment and support, especially on my lowest days. It doesn't seem to matter how one found themselves to be a Mareathoner and even though we are all over the world with different backgrounds and circumstances, there's a definite undercurrent of growth and positivity.

This is not your typical Facebook group. I approve every member. I monitor posts closely. If I am going to be out of town or busy, I ask trusted Mareathoners to monitor for me. In fact, I often remind the group to report any suspicious activity. I've given warnings. I've kicked people out. The group is a safe space where strangers come to ask for support on minor things like mascara or a front entryway storage. A page brimming with confidence, so much so that women pour their hearts out about painful divorces, children being bullied, grief for a lost spouse, and more. The honesty and vulnerability is unmatched; and that feeling is not just online. There are women who have met in the group and then become friends in real life. This warms my heart to no end.

Life's Not a Sprint, It's a Mareathon: I had always wanted a catch phrase, especially when I was on the radio. I love how Ellen Degeneres ends each show with "be kind to one another," and I wanted something of my own. When I was brainstorming ideas for my short-lived cable TV show, I came up with this phrase. Then Jeremy suggested I call the show, *The Mareathon.* It grew from there. It's actually telling that I would choose this as the motto, seeing as I am one of the most impatient people on Earth. I come back to the phrase daily. It reminds us to take a breath and pause. There is no need to sprint through life, running so fast that we don't even enjoy the race. It's more appealing to set a pace and enjoy the road.

Show Up For Others: Mareathoners have shown up for me time and time again. The day before Jeremy died they started posting in the group, asking where I was. They knew something was up because they hadn't heard from me in a few days. After he passed away I would post, "There is no way I could collapse because I feel you all holding me up." It was the absolute truth. Never in my wildest dreams could I have imagined the love and support from every corner of the world. Messages pouring in from people in countless countries, sending love. I asked for videos explaining how Jeremy had touched their lives. I wanted to edit a montage for his funeral to give his family a glimpse into his reach. There ended up being too many videos to include. You can still see this video on my YouTube channel, *Jeremy, In Your Words.*

Leading up to my first Christmas without Jeremy, I shared in a tear-filled video that it had just dawned on me: I wouldn't be able to enjoy my favourite part of the season, my stocking. Ever since I was a little girl, my stocking has been my favourite thing to open. Well, I did not feel alone or go without that Christmas! Gifts started showing up. In DROVES. I got probably ten stockings that Christmas! One was about four feet tall and stuffed with gifts from Mareathoners. I also got package after package of gifts so on-point you would have thought my own mum sent them. These people know me incredibly well. Every gift was so thoughtful and sent with overwhelming love. I was in shock that Christmas, opening gift after gift, in awe of the kindness of strangers on the internet.

I cried a lot that first Christmas. All alone, just me and Thomas. But I never felt lonely. My family may have been thousands of kilometres away, but the Mareathoners were right with me, giving me a hand lotion that I've repurchased so many times I've lost count. Earrings I wear constantly, and every time I place the backing behind the stud, I stand a little taller. I feel a sense of belonging and purpose.

That Christmas I got a message from a Mareathoner named Belinda. She wanted to do something nice for another woman and needed my help. We posted in the group, asking if anyone knew someone locally who was having a tough time and could use a little brightening. We were inundated with names and stories. So Belinda put together four or five different gift baskets and we drove around on Christmas Eve, delivering little pockets of joy to unsuspecting women. It was hands-down, my favourite part of the entire season. One woman said, "You're the only people I'm going to see for the next few days," and another said, "As a single mom, these are the only gifts I am receiving this year." It was incredible perspective and an example of the true spirit of the Mareathoner.

The Arrow: We even have a tattoo. Can you believe that? Me neither. A legit self-imposed, life-long scar. I got an arrow tattoo on my left wrist a few years ago after coming across a saying that an arrow has to be pulled back before it's shot forward into greatness. This serves as a reminder that tough times are preparing you for better days. I loved it so much and got the tattoo. Then Leanne got the tattoo. Then Chelsea did. Then Karlen. Then Alyssa... and it snowballed. More people have gotten this symbol of the Mareathon than I can count. Permanently marking their skin with a reminder to keep going. To persevere. To up-level. That self-care isn't selfish. This melts my heart and propels me to keep going myself.

The Self-High Five: This is something I started saying in my videos after Jeremy died. I wanted to congratulate myself on major obstacles overcome, but also on minor tasks completed. I started doing it, saying it out loud, loving how it made me feel. Why aren't we congratulating ourselves more on the everyday wins? Why are we only counting what we didn't do? Adding to the never-ending to-do list? Screw that. I wanna self-high five! I started doing it so much on camera that it became a running theme. Women started posting their self-high fives in the group, for doing something they'd put off, to standing up for themselves and everything in between. I love seeing women bond with their daughters as Mareathoners and their self-high five wins. Couldn't we all use a little more celebration? It's fun to start to look for things to self-high five, too. Positivity breeds positivity and being proud enough to give a self-high five? More of that please.

You Do You: This main Mareathoner mantra has its own chapter. It represents a reminder to show up for yourself time and time again. You do what is best for you, without apology (as long as you aren't purposely hurting someone else). I'll go into it in more detail later in the book.

When asked who the Mareathoner is, this is how a few members answered:

Tyne said, "*We are strong, resilient, smart, and proud... we aren't afraid to ask for help or show up to help. Deep down we're broken, but we've got those pieces gathered and we Gorilla Glue them back together as often as it takes... the best part... is when we're missing pieces, the others step up and start gluing too.*"

Anna said, "*We've been through a lot, learnt a lot and we care deeply about others. We try hard to remember to care about ourselves, too, and practise self-care.*"

Nicole said, "*A person who recognizes the Mareathon as a committed relationship that will take work and perseverance over a lifetime and discovering along the way that they are capable of more than they ever thought possible.*"

The Mareathon reminds us that we are not alone. If you are reading this, feeling like no one gets you, trust me, they do. You just need to find them. Maybe it's our Mareathoner community and maybe it's another one. Your tribe is out there.

Mareathoners fix my cape by supporting me and supporting each other. They lead by example in their own lives by showing up for themselves and for others, and this inspires me to do the same, giving my cape a quick steam clean when needed. With each hug on the street, we quietly boost each other's capes and as we turn away from each other, the cape flutter is just a little stronger.

Finding Your Cape:

Write out ten things worthy of a self-high five you've done in the last few months. Now just this past week. Now, write out ten things you've done in the last day. Isn't it incredible to see just how much you've accomplished just in one day alone? The more you can identify how much you do to positively enhance your life, the more you will find yourself looking for examples. Our mind focuses on what we allow it to, and the more you look for self-high fives throughout the day, the more you'll find. In an article in the *New York Times,* Dr. Kristin Neff, Associate Professor Humasent and Culture, Educational Psychology Department, University of Texas at Austin, said that her research found that many people don't want to be kind to themselves because they worry about being too self-indulgent. But, being kinder to yourself, according to the research, is also the first step toward being healthier and happier.

Finding reasons to self-high five helps me maintain momentum, especially in the darkest of times. It can be even the smallest things, like remembering to brush my son's teeth or getting him to school on time, which was always Jeremy's job. You can only do your best and some days your best is the bare minimum, and that's okay. As you're about to find out, my momentum has been tested more than once. Life's not a sprint, it's a Mareathon, that's for sure.

CRASH
LANDING

Chapter 5:

Team Unstoppable

JEREMY WAS THE first person I met who truly thought I was funny, and I felt completely comfortable being myself around him. He accepted me for me. Not just accepted me, but deeply loved me. It's because of this that I grew confident to lean into my personality. This support and love quickly became part of my cape as we got to know each other. We were friends first which helped my inexperienced-at-relationships self. It quickly developed into something more and felt so natural. He felt like home. We rarely disagreed. In fact, our first real fight was on his birthday, the first year we were together. He was overwhelmed by my generosity and didn't know how to react. Such a silly fight, in hindsight.

It was so fun that we shared a deep love of music. Even if our tastes varied, music was always on in the house or car, both of us singing along. Early on in our relationship we were driving in the snow and *Wonderwall* by Oasis came on. I remember singing along without noticing the look of shock on his face. He couldn't believe I knew that song as I was more of a Britney Spears and Keith Urban kind of girl! I valued that we both worked in radio. I was a news reporter and he was an on-air announcer at a country music station. I went on to be his news anchor, and his encouragement strengthened my cape as I gained confidence to advance in the industry. We just innately understood what the other person was going through on a rough day. We also got to go on so many fun adventures and we would turn to each other in disbelief that this was 'work'—"they are *paying* us to do this?!?"

A lot of couples have nicknames for each other. We'd both moved to a northern Canadian city where five months of the year it gets down to minus 35 degrees Celsius, and he quickly started calling me Furnace. I have this weird trait of emitting a lot of body heat, even when I feel cold. When I was pregnant, we lovingly referred to Thomas as Space Heater.

Jeremy's nickname was Meatball. How did he get this moniker? Well, we were out on a double date when he choked on a meatball and needed the Heimlich Maneuver to breathe again. No joke! I am mortified to confess to you that I *wasn't* the one to jump up and help him! Date fail. He was fine, we quickly laughed about it and somehow the nickname Meatball stuck. I would dramatically cut up his meatballs into the tiniest bite-sized pieces. My niece even started calling him Uncle Meatball. Furnace and Meatball. It probably sounds weird to you, but it was us. For years, that was us.

Furnace and Meatball became Team Unstoppable. When I decided to move closer to my family, he instantly wanted to join me. Some people closest to him said it was a huge mistake, but we knew this was not just a fling. When I moved away I gave him a card that read, "Together we are unstoppable." We believed nothing could hold us back and that together we could face anything. Furnace and Meatball—Team Unstoppable.

We loved to go on vacation together and travelled to see my brother's family in Philadelphia many times. Jeremy and my brother shared a love of hockey, baseball and music. (Jer loved the Detroit Red Wings and I distinctly remember he was wearing a hockey jersey in the office the first time we met.) They would go to Phillies games and concerts and made sure to get that quintessential Philly Cheesesteak sandwich. We even seriously considered moving closer to my brother and his family once we had kids.

Before we started dating, I knew that Jeremy was hoping our friendship would turn into more. Here's one of my favourite examples of him testing the waters before asking me out: He would come over to watch TV and was always flabbergasted that I didn't own a microwave. How would we make popcorn?! So one evening he brought over a spare microwave he had to my apartment. He set the appliance down on my kitchen counter and excused himself to the restroom. I opened the microwave door and found a gift wrapped inside. I figured he'd left it in there by accident. He shook his head when he came back out and said, "Of course it's for you!" I unwrapped a picture frame to reveal a photo of my favourite view of the lake from my hometown. I was speechless and touched to say the least! I was still grappling with the decision of whether to date a coworker at my first professional radio job, so I just awkwardly hugged him and said thanks. I later learned that Jeremy saw that as his big romantic gesture. Given my response, he had told himself we would never date and to just move on. Later on I asked my boss at the radio station if it was okay if we dated. She laughed and said, of course.

How did I finally know I was ready to move from friendship to relationship with Jer? I called a girlfriend one morning after a night out and simply said, "He dances." She knew that was it. He danced?! My 21-year-old self saw this as very important. I also loved that he was following his passion of music by pursuing a career in radio. He wasn't in it for the money (no one is in radio for that!), but rather he'd found what he was meant to do. I was impressed that he moved so far away from home for his first job that it took two days to drive there.

Our first place together was a one-bedroom, 600-square--foot apartment, with zero space and barely above ground. Like so small I used to do my makeup over the kitchen garbage! But we loved it. It's where we figured out how to live together. It's where he made countless cooked breakfasts, which were his specialty. First he made the Five Star, consisting of five parts: hash browns, eggs, bacon, toast, and OJ. Then he upgraded to the "Bacon and Egg McGoran." A bacon and egg sandwich on an English muffin. He even had a little round silicon contraption to make the egg a perfect circle. One breakfast memory definitely stands out: while we were still in our pajamas, him sporting a Simpsons t-shirt, he got down on one knee beside our bed and asked me to be his wife.

We were married the next year and flew to Jamaica for our honeymoon. We secretly had an extra day before departing on our honeymoon, but told all our wedding guests we were flying out the morning after! (Sorry if you're reading this and were included in that white lie!) We had the most lovely, relaxing couple of days to recover from the wedding before boarding our plane to Jamaica. The weather was perfect, the sands white and the ocean water as clear as could be. We ate jerk chicken every day, switching between piña coladas and tequila sunrises to wash it down. Bliss. Pure bliss.

Jeremy was reliable, hard-working, and loyal. To hear his voice, you'd instantly assume he talked for a living. It boomed with confidence and sheer volume, usually unbeknownst to him. His laugh was infectious and easy. He was also tidy. I never had to nag him about leaving his socks on the floor. This is funny to me because Thomas' classmates often comment how tidy *he* is. We may have disagreed on what a clean house was, but he was always tidy. For years I would come home after a wine night with the girls and laugh to him that I never had anything to contribute in the "complaining about our boyfriends" portion of the evening. People would often comment how perfect of a fit we seemed, and we felt it too.

Jeremy loved our nieces and nephew unconditionally and, in seeing that, I knew he was ready to be a parent. When we first started dating, Jer was on the fence about having kids. He met my niece a few months later and on the drive home couldn't stop gushing about how great she was and how much he wanted to have a family, too. Our nieces and nephew loved him as well, crawling all over him, excitedly asking him to play or read to them. He took his role as uncle seriously, loving those kids and always crouching down to their level, ready for whatever game or adventure they concocted. Jeremy would sit down in the radio studio and read aloud children's books, sending our niece and nephew the audio recordings for Christmas. They still ask to listen to those stories to this day.

He was incredibly attentive and supportive once I became pregnant with Thomas. We were so excited to start a family, planning our life together as parents. He was forever getting me slurpees and popsicles to satisfy my cravings, even in the middle of winter! He came to the prenatal classes, we hired a doula, and Jer was right by my side throughout the incredibly tough labour. The second Thomas was born, he wrapped his fingers around Jer's. They were linked, immediately. Jeremy chose his name too: Thomas after my dad and his middle name, Nelson, is Jeremy's mom's maiden name.

We were never the perfect couple, different in many ways, but it was us. He was supportive of my crazy ideas, especially when I was ready to end my successful radio career to start my own business. He was always happy to be in a video, take a photo or help me talk out a problem. Friends would comment how they loved the way we would stop whatever we were doing when the other person got home, to say hello with a hug and a kiss. We'd never thought about it, but it came naturally.

It took almost ten years for me to realize there had been warning signs that Jeremy was struggling with anxiety. The signs were peppered throughout our relationship, but hindsight is 20/20 as they say. We'd been dating for a year and went on vacation together to see my brother in Philadelphia. We spent a few days in New York City and while at lunch the first day, I went to use the restroom. When I returned, the table was empty. My purse was sitting there and he was gone. I was stunned and shocked, wondering what kind of weird joke he was playing. A few panic-stricken moments later, he returned and told me he had gotten sick. I was pretty upset. He had left my purse at the table in New York! But the city made him really nervous and overwhelmed. He managed to shake it off and we had a great visit, subsequently returning to the city many times.

The same thing happened a few years later in Las Vegas. We got there and he almost immediately threw up. I had forgotten about the first time in New York, faded from memory. But on this trip his anxiety was worse, leaving him stressed and upset many times. These panic attacks increased and he was often anxious.

Through work in therapy, Jer realized that his anxiety had started in his teens and it had been building for so long. A multitude of life stressors crescendoed and he saw our doctor for medication. I don't know how long he'd had suicidal thoughts, but he first confessed them to me a year and a half before he died. His panic was contagious, and I lived in constant fear that he would hurt himself. I tried to do anything and everything to make his life as easy as possible. Our therapist told me to let him in and share the load, but I just couldn't. I was terrified—and on the edge of a breakdown. I felt trapped with no way to resolve what was happening. It was like being in a sinkhole of panic at all times. I was suffocating and my health suffering.

Our love struggled to stay afloat. We tried to laugh and have moments of reprieve, but things had shifted. We were no longer a partnership. He was crumbling, his mental health at a new level of darkness. My handsome, boisterous husband was spiralling further into depression and anxiety. I was collapsing, trying to carry the load. It tore through our marriage, uninvited, but nevertheless bulldozed a place for itself at the table and in our bed and never left.

Furnace and Meatball. Team Unstoppable. I'll never regret taking a chance on the boy in the hockey jersey. There would be no Thomas without Jeremy. No Mareathon. I'd be a completely different person. He changed and shaped me in so many ways that I could fill an entirely new book. Just know that to know me is to know the imprint left on my heart by that man. It was inspiring to watch him turn his pain into a public message, a warning for others. I know for a fact that

Jeremy's bravery and honesty saved countless lives as he spoke about his mental health battle. I still get messages from people around the world talking about him and how he's influenced their journey.

I wish he was here to see that impact to truly know the legacy he left. He may not know it, but I do.

Chapter 6:

We Can All Learn From This

"**J**UST TELL ME," he pleaded to me. "Just say the words. It's over, isn't it?"

He stood six feet away from me, in our basement. I felt like I was going to pass out.

"I am so sorry, Jer. I am so sorry."

As soon as the words escaped my lips I collapsed on my knees into the worst, gut-wrenching sobs I'd ever experienced. For two years, I had been crying almost every day in private, but nothing like this.

I'd ended our marriage.

On June 7, 2017, I told Jeremy that it was over. I know the date, because two days later he killed himself. My worst nightmare came true.

***

Before this day, we had many lengthy conversations about being the modern family: we could both find someone else and be co-parents. Maybe this could work. We had days upon days, and hours upon hours of conversations about this.

But when it came down to it, Jeremy didn't think he could function without me and I had created an environment where this was easy to believe: a codependent relationship with unhealthy patterns. I was guilty, for sure. I did everything because it was easier. I tried to always be one or two steps ahead to ease his day, smooth the edges, and make things as simple as possible for him as his anxiety and depression deepened. It's what many women would do if their husbands were struggling. You pick up the slack, expecting the scal/es to tip back at some point, but they never did.

The day he died, Jeremy was going to stay with his family, five hours away. Our therapist had recommended he get support from family as we came to grips with our separation. After dropping Thomas off at school, I went out for a therapy appointment and then to test drive cars. We had been sharing one vehicle for a couple of years and Thomas and I would be without wheels once Jeremy was with his parents.

The last time I saw Jeremy, there was no indication of what was to come. He reminded me to submit the receipts to get reimbursed for Thomas' Autism therapy equipment. There was no signal, no sign, no emotional goodbye with Thomas. Jer barely said goodbye to his son that morning. I remember having to physically push him to give Thomas a hug. He was detaching before my eyes. Little did I know that he had written a suicide note and was preparing to leave our house in just a couple of hours, never to return.

That afternoon, my mum picked up Thomas from school and called me to say that the van was parked at home and Jeremy's suitcase was still there. That's when I knew, *this was it.* Not wanting to believe my worst fears, I frantically texted and called him over and over, begging him to pick up the phone.

Walking along the sidewalk, as if in slow motion, I turned the corner and coincidentally ran into a friend. We had plans to see each other later that day, but she could hear the fear in my voice and started walking with me. My mum picked us up and, when we got into the house, I raced around knowing I would find a note. I scrambled up the stairs and into our bedroom. I screamed. There it was on his bedside table.

I called 911. We texted everyone we knew, asking if they had heard from him, seen him at all. News was starting to spread, with police and Search and Rescue coming in and out of the house, helicopters flying overhead. At one point that evening, the police had said they were going to put the news about Jeremy missing on social media, but it never appeared.

It didn't have to. They had found him.

He had brought only his ID with him, not his wallet or phone. Later, picking up his items at the RCMP station, I realized this was not a snap decision. He had researched what to do, planned all the details. Wiped his computer search history clean. The suicide note had clearly been folded over and over, for who knows how long.

***

Part of his suicide note read, "Mare this is not your fault. I am sorry but the pain is too much."

I am trying to offer you takeaways from each of the experiences I have had, that you can apply to your own life. This is obviously a difficult chapter to write. I walked away from these words for weeks. There are no steps of action to recommend. There was literally nothing anybody could have done. I supported Jeremy for years, doing everything I could possibly imagine to help him. He went to therapy, did yoga, went vegan, quit his job, went on medication and tried everything he could to overcome the beast of mental health.

Many people we know believe that if it wasn't that day, it would have been the next month, or next year.

There was nothing anyone of us could have done.

I remember the stream of people coming up to me the week after and saying, "I should have called him, I should have picked up the phone, I should have come to get him. I should have... I should have..." I was struggling so much with these comments and questions, and finally asked my therapist what to say.

Her advice? We can all learn from this.

It was no one's fault, but we can all learn from this.

Chapter 7:

Disclaimer: It's Not Here

I F YOU'RE SCANNING the pages of this book looking for the chapter on "How to Save My Spouse (or Friend, Child, Parent, etc.)," it's not here.

One of the most frequently asked questions I got after Jeremy killed himself was: "Mare, what did you miss? What signs did you not see? What happened leading up to that day? I don't want to miss what you did."

It felt as if people thought I'd turned a blind eye to the man I loved who was deeply troubled and who I cared for 24/7. It was as if they were saying that I KNEW my husband was going to walk out of our house on the morning of June 9, 2017 and never return. It was as if I'd let him do it. This line of questioning made me feel as if I was to blame.

For years I thought it was my job to protect Jeremy and save his life. I thought if I just stayed a few steps ahead, made his life as soft around the edges as I could, he'd be okay.

What I've learned is: you can't force a cape on anyone else. You can't sew it for them or super glue it to their shoulders. You can only save yourself.

If you know someone who is suffering, encourage them to seek professional help. Start with their doctor. Get them a mental health assessment. Encourage them to talk to a therapist. To take medication prescribed by their doctor if needed.

To exercise. To eat better. To take care of themselves. Be there for the ones you love. Support them. Make sure they know they are not alone.

But it is not on you to save them. I carried the weight of keeping my husband alive for years. And yet, here I am, a widow, writing this book. Nothing I did saved Jeremy. There were no signs or signals that his end had come.

If you're looking for the chapter on how to save someone, it's not here. What you will find are specific ways I strengthened my cape to save myself—and how you can, too.

NAVIGATING TO THE LIGHT

Chapter 8:

It's Going to Get Worse Before It Gets Better

Ｉｆ Ｉ ｃｏｕｌｄ ｇｏ back and write a letter to my previous self, five years ago, this is what I would say:

Mare,

I wish I could hug you and ease your racing heart. Urge you to take a deep breath even though your chest is so tight it feels physically impossible to do so. Your lungs are constricted by panic, anxiety, and immense sadness.

I know you feel there is no hope, no light, and no way out.

I promise there is. I promise this pain will subside. I promise you will get through this. In fact, you already are. I promise.

I know you are wondering how you got here, obsessing over the choices you've made, retracing your steps, and desperately looking for an answer. Know that everything you've done and every pivot you've made is leading you to an unimaginable life with love, joy, light, and peace.

I'm sorry to tell you that right now there is no easy answer. There ARE answers and you WILL find them, but not quite yet. You already hold the tools to not only endure what's to come, but thrive.

One day you will realize that you no longer cry every time you're alone in the car. That you aren't crying yourself to sleep. That you're able to take a deep breath without it catching in your chest, escaping only as a surprised sob.

It will happen again, I promise. You have to trust me on this.

You believe that no one could possibly understand your pain and that no one could ever imagine what you are going through. But guess what? There are countless people in this world who have been through their version of your current hell, unfortunately. And they have made it out, some even thriving. Start sharing your story more in videos, on the air and online. You will find your tribe. Parents of children with special needs are all around you. Please tell people what is happening at home. Please open up. I know you think that your family is too busy or doesn't want to be bothered by your saga. Guess what? It's the opposite. They want to be let in and they want you to dissolve the walls you shot up the day Thomas got his hearing aids. They are peering in from the other side, wanting to knock a window into your world, but are often too scared to take action. Yes, they are busy and have their own things to contend with, but if you open up and give them the chance to respond, they will.

You feel that you can't tell anyone except your inner circle how bad things are with Jeremy. You don't want to disrespect him. You don't want to rock the boat. You do not need to suffer in silence. Let your internal screams make their way to the surface. You have a wonderful group of people in your life who wonder why you are so upset, closed off, and why you redirect their questions all the time. TELL THEM. You think that people (i.e., your family and friends, even those who are the closest) know how bad things are with Jeremy. They don't. Reaching out and sharing your truth is not gossiping. It's accepting a life raft.

You believe that you are responsible for keeping him alive. You are not. YOU ARE NOT. I'm going to repeat this until somehow it sinks beneath your flesh and into your soul. You. Are. Not. Responsible. Only he is responsible for his life. No one else. You've taken on his happiness, making sure he's comfortable and that everything around him is white noise. This is unhealthy. You deserve to be supported. Who is supporting YOU? It's not okay that you are not supported as you need. It's not okay that you are holding up the house. This is not okay. You know this. You know it's not okay and you feel there is no alternative. There is. Only he is responsible for his happiness and you for yours. Start spending more time on what makes you happy and set boundaries with him. He needs to know when you are upset. He needs to know how hard this is on you. Start speaking up. Stop letting things go because it's making you resentful.

You are highly affected by other people's energy. You are an empath, or what your therapist calls a "super feeler." You know that the vibe in your home (low, dark, angry, uneasy, negative) is making you incredibly uncomfortable, to put it mildly. You are not responsible for making the room light and positive. You do not have to try to regulate the energy in the room. If he is angry or upset or sad or down or guilty or jealous... that is not on you.

What is your responsibility? YOU, DAMNIT.

The sooner you make sleep a priority, the better. Go to bed early. Share the overnight Thomas shifts with Jeremy. This is not only on you. It's on both of you. Find magnesium oil and use it to help you sleep. Do yoga at night. Read books. Watch light-hearted shows. Move your body. START MEDITATING. Meditation is going to change your life. Start now. Like now. Stop pushing aside your needs to tiptoe around Jeremy.

Stop worrying that you are disappointing others. Babe, you are amazing and your voice is important. You may feel like it never has been, but it is. Your opinions are important. Your story is going to save lives. Speak up and don't worry about the people who seem to judge you. That says more about them and less about you. Honestly. You aren't for everyone and that's okay.

You are confused. You are conflicted. You did not expect this. You wonder why you feel so uneasy so often. You feel like you can't breathe sometimes because you are so out of your skin with pain.

You feel guilty for even being upset. You think, "How dare I be upset when I don't have special needs or am suicidal? Get a grip! This is not about me!" You don't dare focus on yourself in order to give the illusion of positivity and strength. And yet, you feel yourself chipping away every day as you mask excruciating pain. You sob silent tears while reading the newscast on the morning show, only allowing audible cries once the microphone is off. This is not okay. You wipe the tears, take a breath, and carry on, laughing about Britney Spears with your co-host. He is paralyzed with a mix of emotions for you, although you've sworn him to secrecy, asking him to treat you like anyone else, desperate for a sliver of normalcy.

You will not always be in this fight-or-flight mode. Lean on people. Let them in. Your pain is valid. Your feelings are valid.

You feel alone. You are not. Asking for help is not a sign of weakness or an imposition. Think of how much you like to help others and the joy it brings you. Let someone else feel that joy. It may not be the people you expect who will help you, but help is just waiting in the wings nonetheless. It is your job to ask for it.

Jeremy does love you. You know this. You love him. You didn't invite this vicious third wheel of unmanageable mental health into your marriage, but it's here and it's not going anywhere. That is not a reflection on you. It is not your fault. You cannot fix it. But what you can do is focus on yourself and your mindset.

I have some not-so-good news: it's going to get a hell of a lot worse. Before it gets better, it's going to get a lot worse.

Look at your tattoo, "There is only love," and this will carry you. Love for you, for Thomas, and for Jeremy. Love for the journey and for the universe wanting what's best for you, even when you can't see the big picture. You've always known you were destined for something out of the ordinary, well that is true. With greatness comes struggle. I'd tell you what you need to know, but the best part of all is that you already know it. It's all right inside of you already. Your positivity, your courage, your love for your husband and son, your incredible strength... it's all right there.

You've got this.

You can do anything for ten minutes.

Life's not a sprint, it's a Mareathon. Your Mareathon is taking you places you can't imagine.

You're ready.

oxox M

Chapter 9:

Vulnerability Stitches the Cape

I CAN HEAR WHAT you are thinking: Be vulnerable? No, thanks Mare. I'd rather get a full Brazilian bikini wax while reliving my last break-up, listening to a symphony of nails on the chalkboard.

No, thank you.

Just thinking about vulnerability is enough to make our skin crawl and have us build up walls before we realize what's happening.

Dr. Brene Brown, a research professor at the University of Houston Graduate College of Social Work, describes vulnerability and authenticity as lying at the root of human connection. She says in her research she's found that vulnerability in others is revered as courageous, but vulnerability in ourselves is often seen as weakness.

But the secret I am here to tell you, from experience over and over again, is that vulnerability truly sets you free. It is far from a sign of weakness. It will make that cape flutter in the wind like nobody's business.

Here's an example of me being the opposite of vulnerable: When Thomas received his hearing loss diagnosis, I emailed our family to share the news. He failed the mandatory hearing test in the hospital the day after he was born, but the midwives assured us it was common. Then, he failed another test a few days later. Then another. We were sent an hour away for the most upsetting and frustrating testing sessions which involved my newborn having to be silent and completely still for hours on end in a dark room, hooked up to a machine that measured his internal reaction to sound. It was traumatizing, to say the least. Thomas was diagnosed with progressive hearing loss and fitted for hearing aids at four months old. My world spun out of control, as if I was having an out-of-body experience. In an email to our family, I explained his diagnosis, sternly scolding anyone who dreamed about pitying Thomas.

In hindsight, I feel that I built a stiff wall between us and our families with that message. Jeremy and I often felt alone in the years after Thomas was born as his hearing loss rapidly progressed and his Autism emerged. We were in fight-or-flight mode to the maximum. We were terrified and felt isolated. On the outside was the façade that we were doing great, so people weren't worried. But the first four years of Thomas' life were increasingly terrifying with every appointment and overwhelming diagnosis. We were panicked that people would judge our beautiful son, so we were proactively defensive.

I don't regret how things went, because it was an unimaginable time of survival for our family. But I now see that, by not being vulnerable, we shut people out and didn't even give them the chance to be supportive.

In an attempt to learn coping skills to deal with Thomas' diagnosis, Jeremy and I started seeing a marriage counsellor. During the first appointment she stressed, "You need to ask for help." We never wanted to be a burden and felt that so many people in our lives were already dealing with a heavy load themselves. So we continued on the island of our own making, maintaining the appearance of strength. When we would ask for help, often times we felt brushed off because people believed that façade.

In November of 2014, our lives shifted in a big way. As radio hosts, Jeremy and I shared our lives with our listeners, but neither of us had ever spoken publicly about Thomas' special needs. Yes, I had been actively posting videos and photos of our little guy online, but I'd never addressed his hearing loss or Autism diagnosis. Thomas started going to his first set of Autism therapy appointments at the local child development centre, and at the same time they were getting ready to host a fundraising telethon. I felt compelled to tell our story with the hope that radio listeners would donate.

The night before I went public I was a nervous wreck, asking people online to be gentle when they heard our story on the next show. Even the general manager of the station had no idea of Thomas' dual diagnosis. The next morning, my co-host and good friend helped me reveal Thomas' diagnosis to our audience for the first time. It's the first time I remember openly crying on the air. I sobbed. All I hoped to achieve was a few extra donations for the telethon.

What happened next stunned me.

As soon as we turned off the microphones and started playing a song, people flooded the studio with calls. My supervisor, who had been incredibly generous with Jeremy and I the past few years with time off and understanding emergencies with T, came in and hugged me. The executive director of the child development centre came rushing into the radio station, thanking me for sharing about our son. Emotional and in shock at what I had just done, I politely thanked everyone.

Then the messages started. I was inundated with hundreds of messages from listeners and YouTube subscribers providing support and sharing their stories of similar experiences. In opening up to tell our story, others felt compelled to share theirs. By the hundreds.

This was my first glimpse into how vulnerability sets you free. I was emotional telling our story on the air that day because, with every word and revelation, I felt a crippling weight lift. This was no longer something to hide or defend. This was our beautiful son and I was going to proudly share his story. Being open about Thomas' special needs has educated thousands of people on inclusivity, Autism, hearing loss, cochlear implants, and more. I want people to see that we love Thomas without limitations or parameters. It opened us up to educating our family and friends as well as strangers about special needs. We'd happily answer questions in the grocery store and online.

And a couple of months later, we'd do it again. One terrifying day Jeremy called me the minute my show ended and said, "You need to come home right now. I want to hurt myself and I am scared of what I am about to do." I rushed home immediately, taking him to see our therapist and doctor one after the other that day. He took much-needed medical leave and came back on the air just as our company was preparing for a mental health awareness day. It was the first time the station had done this initiative and Jeremy felt it was as good a time as any to share. So, Jer turned on his microphone and went public about his struggles with mental health. He found the same thing: vulnerability set him free. When colleagues or friends or family members asked him why he'd taken medical leave, he was completely honest. In turn, he was shocked at how many people in his social circle came back with, "Me too, man." He realized people he worked beside every day were also struggling with their own mental health. He felt supported and less alone by being vulnerable and speaking his truth.

As a side note, I feel compelled to tell you that this was 2015, a time in which mental health was rarely talked about publicly. It was still considered very taboo, and I am happy to see this has changed rapidly in the years since. We still have a long way to go to make it a non-issue, but I wholeheartedly believe Jeremy was a pioneer, instrumental in boosting the conversation.

Jer also learned the hard way that being vulnerable can make certain people very uncomfortable. He had some friends turn away and distance themselves from him as talking openly about mental health made things awkward. This was incredibly hurtful, but he also saw other friendships strengthen because of his honesty. When you are authentically yourself and show vulnerability, others are drawn to that. I now know this to be one of the best shared experiences.

When I started my social media marketing business, I was nervous about sharing our mental health journey online. I was worried that potential clients would shy away from working with me, when in reality, the opposite happened. People sought me out, confessing their own struggles or someone they loved as they asked to work with me. I don't doubt that there were people scared of my openness, but you'll never be everyone's cup of tea, and that is just fine with me.

Being authentic and bravely vulnerable has changed my life. It's also taught me a valuable lesson: Everyone is either going through something or has been through it. E-v-e-r-y-o-n-e. It's been an honour to have complete strangers pour their hearts out to me, feeling a kinship as we stand in authentic vulnerability together. When you start to share, as scary as it is, you'll find commonalities with people you never knew existed.

Realizing that everyone has a story and has been through it provides a healthy reality check. When you're feeling sorry for yourself, thinking there is no way that anyone could possibly have it as bad as you, look around and remind yourself that they do. In fact, someone has it much worse. Also, someone also has been through exactly the battle you're currently in and made the most of it. One of my main goals is to ensure people know they aren't alone. I have felt my loneliest in dark times and I want to save someone from that dark pain. Vulnerability turns on a light and that sets you free. It can fly you towards a light shining on others around you who are dealing with the same thing, who have fought their own battles that have battered and beaten their own cape.

The nerves that come with stepping into your truth are normal. I can tell you that I felt a massive weight on my chest every day I wasn't open about our struggles. I was ashamed. I was petrified. I was sick at the thought of people judging our family, thinking less of us. But guess what? Some people did and that's okay. Others saw my truth, stepped into it with me and that's an unparalleled feeling.

Vulnerability sets you free.

How to Stitch the Cape

Find Someone Safe to Talk To:

If you're aching to feel that release of vulnerability, but are understandably terrified, here is my advice. Find someone with whom you feel safe. Someone you know who will listen without judgement. A safe place to start can be a doctor or a therapist. That's what both Jeremy and I did. Like I said, we started out with counselling after Thomas was diagnosed with Autism, but then we both ended up seeing our own therapists separately. My therapists listened without judgement and always made me realize that I wasn't alone in how I was feeling. They gave me invaluable tools to not only get through the day-to-day, but also make the big life decisions. I recommend everyone seek therapy at some point in their lives.

Take Stock of Your Peers:

If you don't feel comfortable sharing yourself with them in an honest and vulnerable way, they may be holding you back from stepping into your truth. Like I said, being vulnerable and being yourself can come with a price. But when you lose friends who don't support you, well, are they really worth holding on to?

This takes practice. I realized that even though I am happy being vulnerable with people, I was holding back when I felt my circumstances were too much for others to handle. As we reached the second anniversary of Jeremy's death, I was slipping back into feeling like a burden. My good friend told me, "It's not your place to decide whether I can handle something. You need to tell me what's up and then it's up to me to decide." I'd never had it explained that way. I had been turning away and pushing her away, thinking she was already stressed and couldn't possibly have the space to listen to me cry. But, in pushing her away, she was more hurt. Her honesty and vulnerability in telling me her feelings made me realize I was doing that to other people in my life as well. This realization has strengthened many of my relationships with both friends and family.

It's not up to us to decide if others can handle our vulnerability. We must simply present ourselves and stay true to that, regardless of other people's reactions.

Start Small:

Feel it out. Test the waters. You'll find that tribe. And you'll also realize that aspects of your life and growth will be received differently depending on the person. You may also find that someone in your life who is also struggling may not be receptive to certain things. Be gentle with them. If you expect to be loved without parameters, you'd better be ready to give love the same way. (This is in no way me telling you to stick around when the relationship turns toxic.)

Maybe you have a burning desire to try out a new hobby, but are worried about people judging you. Find a group involved with that hobby. These may end up being your people. Maybe you've found yourself in a toxic relationship and feel stuck. Tell someone. Someone who will listen and help you. Gravitate towards those who love you without parameters and show them the same respect in return.

To this day I get nervous before I post something super vulnerable online or share it in a video. There's a little doubtful voice inside of me wanting to put up that wall just like I did in 2011 after Thomas was fitted for his first teeny, tiny hearing aids. But I remind myself that whatever I am feeling is shared by many other people. I am not alone and with each act of courageous vulnerability, the pieces of my cape are stitched closer together, seamlessly fused with a stitch my nana (the expert sewer) would have admired.

Vulnerability builds strength and the more you step into your truth, the stronger and more free you become. A weight will lift as you share your authentic truth. Eventually, it starts to take less energy to be authentic than it does to be anything else.

Finding Your Cape:

Let the pen explain how you're feeling. Answer the following questions:

★ With whom do I feel safe being vulnerable?
★ What do I want to share?
★ Are there people in my life who judge my openness?
★ Am I creating a safe space for my loved ones to be vulnerable?
★ How do I react when someone else bravely shares with me?
★ What am I hoping to achieve in being vulnerable?
★ How does being vulnerable make me feel?
★ What positive results have I seen from being vulnerable?

Chapter 10:

Give It Six Months

D O YOU STRUGGLE with change? I have always thrived on it. Craved it, in fact. As a young girl, I would constantly change the décor in my room with homemade collages created from teen magazines and hung with blue sticky tack. I had a deep love of inspirational quotes and pop culture, with a draw to cute boys and powerful women. (Some things never change!) I loved to rearrange the furniture, constantly looking for ways to make things feel fresh and new. Being able to change and adapt are skills that were instilled in me at a young age as we moved four times before my tenth birthday. I have been in my current home for eleven years, the longest I've ever lived in one place. A couple years after we moved in I was ready to sell and change it up. Itching for a change. I've always wanted to be moving forward and working to up-level. I get that from my dad. He constantly moved our family from town to town as he furthered his career as a school teacher.

After I graduated high school, I moved away to live with my aunt and uncle while enrolled in university. I absolutely loved living with them, and it was incredible to have that time getting to know them. That was the highlight. But school? Not for me. I hated it, and that's no exaggeration. I realized quickly that I wasn't interested in being at school to figure out what I wanted to do professionally. I didn't see the purpose in my classes. What job was Canadian history or philosophy going to get me? When I came home for Thanksgiving, I cried for three days straight, begging my parents to let me drop out of university. My mum says it was incredibly difficult to watch me so tormented and unhappy. My dad gave me great advice that weekend. He said that he'd struggled in his past, immigrating to Canada in his early twenties to start a new life for himself. It was scary and difficult, but he came up with a strategy to help him adapt. He said to never judge anything or make a decision before giving it six months. Most things are scary at the beginning, especially when you are reaching out of your comfort zone and up-levelling. I went back to school, finished the semester, and did make it through that first year of university, but didn't go back for second year. I have carried that six-month rule with me through so many tough choices. After finishing broadcast journalism school, I moved far away from my family, first love, and friends for my first paid radio gig. I was scared and lonely. About six weeks in, a job opening came up not too far from my hometown and I was tempted to apply. But I thought of my dad and wanted to give this adventure a fair shot. As it turns out, if I had left to take that job closer to home, I never would have dated Jeremy who worked at the same station.

Part of being proficient at adapting is giving it time and space to unfold. "Life's not a sprint, it's a Mareathon." You will need to show yourself grace and patience as you adapt. Change is HARD and it can be frustrating as you find your way. The last thing you need is your inner critic whispering harsh, judgemental words to you. That's where the cape comes in.

Grace, patience, and self-love are all woven throughout your cape. Show yourself grace by acknowledging that nothing worthwhile comes without struggle. Also, no one successful ever got it perfect on the first try. Give yourself patience and self-love by remembering this. Add some self-high fives for every baby step along the way. Your cape gains strength when you show yourself these wonderful character traits. With this strength, the cape, in turn, protects and propels you. You'll hear whispers of confidence and reminders to be patient rolling in from your back. Your life is unfolding as it should; you can let go and trust as you ease into a big life change.

According to an article on the Mind Tools website, studies show people deal with changes in one of two ways, "escape coping" or "control coping." Escape coping means you work hard to avoid the difficulties of change, like avoiding meetings or purposely forgetting to sign paperwork. Control coping is what we are looking for. It's preparing you to propel. You're not acting like a victim but instead the superhero wearing the cape that you are, taking things as they come and proactively dealing with them.

Some of us need to work on being adaptable, and that's okay. Often we are resistant to change as a form of self-protection. Start small. Rearrange your living room. Take a different way to work. Try a new recipe. Get out of your comfort zone just a little, and then start to do it more often. It's a trait that needs to be exercised, and making little changes is a good way to build your comfort with adapting. Paint a wall. Change the photos in the frames. Book a trip to experience new scenery.

Work to approach any change, no matter the scale, with positivity. Go into it with an open mind, instead of expecting the worst. You've got this! Your cape has your back. Remember that change happens over time and the more monumental the life shift, the more time you need to give it. My dad said six months. Maybe you'll need a longer trial run. And that's okay.

When it comes to tough change, acceptance is key. It's also usually the difficult part. Being the parent of a child with special needs is a constant game of adaptation, but I accept Thomas for who he is and help as best I can to give him a loving quality of life. Is it hard? That's putting it mildly. Every day is different and I have no roadmap of his future, let alone what things will be like in a month from now. He watches me adapt calmly, and he follows suit. It's imperative to remember that our children watch our every move and behaviour. Set a good example.

At some point when you make a big decision resulting in change, you need to ride the waves. No judgement. No white-knuckling. No second-guessing. When you inevitably have those moments of panic or self-doubt, listen to your cape. It will remind you of your goal, where you've been, and the power you have to persevere. I had never planned to start my own business. This was never my plan. But there came a time in my life when I needed to leave radio. I figured out how to adapt and best provide for my family. Easy? Nope. Secure? Nope. Worthwhile? Hell, yes. It wasn't a decision I made lightly or quickly. In fact it was the result of years of reflection, research, and brainstorming. When your intent is pure, positive, and progressive, then the change doesn't seem as terrifying. When you can come back to why you're making these changes, adapting and accepting can be more palatable.

Hard change is HARD and we need to acknowledge that. Don't pretend that it's all easy and positive and fabulous. The best things happen out of our comfort zones and never come easily.

Becoming a single parent has been arguably the most significant change in my life. Almost every day seems to have a new dip or turn in the road, something to navigate. How do I adapt? One day at a time. Sometimes one minute at a time. Every night as I collapse into bed, I physically self-high five to congratulate myself for making it through a new day of change. One day it will feel like normal, but not yet. So I take it one thing at a time.

Tips to Make Changes Easier:

- ★ Be kind to yourself and mindful of your self talk
- ★ Make daily gratitude lists. I do this out loud, while driving
- ★ Celebrate the little wins and victories along the way, no matter how seemingly insignificant—get in some daily self-high fives
- ★ Give it six months before judging
- ★ Stop white-knuckling and ride the wave
- ★ Take it one day or one minute at a time, with grace and patience
- ★ Remind yourself of the alternative: not moving forward doesn't do anyone any good

Finding Your Cape:

When struggling with the idea of making a change, we want to train our minds to see whatever positives are possible in the situation. I get it. Sometimes this is excruciatingly difficult. You've been dumped or fired or suffered unimaginable loss. Find positive? Yeah right! I realize that they may be seemingly insignificant, but *any* positives, make the list. I am serious. *Any* positive will do. After Jeremy took his life, this is what my list of positives looked like on any given day:

- ★ I can breathe
- ★ I can hear
- ★ I can walk
- ★ I can afford my home
- ★ I can feed my son and myself
- ★ I have a car that makes me feel safe
- ★ I have a great support network
- ★ The sky is blue
- ★ My country is safe
- ★ Thomas is happy

See? I am not kidding when I say list *any* positives you can. If it's a big change like a move, break it down into little steps. Make it so it seems as though *anything* is doable. Because, well, it is.

Be kind to yourself and allow yourself space to adapt, shift, and adjust. In finding the positives every day, even in a scary time like a move, a break-up or losing someone, you will start to look for the good instead of focusing on the negative. I find that being adaptable is a skill like a muscle, something you must continue to work at strengthening.

The more you purposely find gratitude in the little things, the more you will hear those lists whispered back to you by your cape. As it's secured tightly to your shoulders when you're in the thick of making changes, it will remind you to see the good, the positive and the future. Clever secret weapon, isn't it?

Chapter 11

Do Some Sh*t:
An Interlude

H I, TOUGH-LOVE MARE here. I don't come out very often. Well, I am always around, but just in her head, pushing her.

You want to know how I get so much done in a day? Meet Tough-Love Mare. She doesn't come out much because I worry she'd come across as pushy or too much.

But this is my book, so here she is.

(She has a potty mouth TBH.)

One of my biggest pet peeves has always been people who complain about things, but don't do anything to fix the issue.

DO. SOMETHING.

Always. No matter what you are facing there is *always* something to DO. We can reflect all we want and meditate and exercise and drink lemon water. All of this is wonderful and I recommend you do it on the daily. But then what?!

DO SOME SHIT. Please. For the love of everything that is good, and for the sake of the bomb-ass future waiting for you, do something.

Start. Just start. Summon that cape and do the work. This doesn't happen to me often, because anyone who follows me knows that I work very hard. But once in a while, someone will lament that everything comes easy to me and that they wish they had some of that luck.

Sorry, but luck is kind of bullshit.

You can win the lottery, but without goals and your head on straight, you're going to piss that money away and be right back where you started.

I've heard super successful celebs say they are just lucky. I don't believe it. No one gets to a high level without hard work, hustle, and manifestation. Every. Damn. Day. Don't tell me that it's just being in the right place at the right time. You've worked hard to get your ass to that place because you DID SOMETHING.

I've muted and unfollowed so many people on social media, some close friends, because they are forever posting a whiny status, complaining, and playing the victim. I could have easily slipped into that category when I became a widow, but I continually resisted the urge. Of course being a widow is awful and I've wallowed, feeling helpless many times, privately. But, I know that Jeremy would want me to move forward and to find strength. He'd want me to maintain momentum and take action to process my grief instead of posting attention-seeking comments online.

According to research from the University of Minnesota, negative attitudes can result in chronic stress, which upsets the body's hormone balance and damages the immune system. This can lead to high blood pressure, heart disease, digestive issues, and more.

Stop playing the victim. Stop looking for pity. Stop expecting someone else to fix your shit.

Only you can control your place in life, your mindset and your future.

Only you.

So, whatcha gonna do about it?

That's right. You're going to DO SOMETHING. Think of your to-do list lining the cape. It's flowing with you and with every tick of a box, the cape helps you gain momentum.

Figure out what the problem is. Make a list of everything that is bothering you, that keeps you up at night and that you want to change. Then make subcategories under each problem. Prioritize them in order. Make a plan for each and then get to work. When things were at their lowest for me, I made lists in my journal of what I wanted to work on, usually the categories of home, family, marriage, work, health, friends, etc. I'd write down what I wanted. This is the key. I started to move away from what was wrong and instead I would imagine where I wanted to be. How I wanted to live and love. I'd picture my home, my life, my work, friends, and more.

Want to know a fun fact? I was terrified to go back to my old journals from a few years ago when I was researching this book. I was worried that it would send me right back to that place. Instead, I read the pen strokes of a woman who was hurting but still strong as hell and determined to fix her life. She knew four years ago that the future was bright and she was hell-bent on getting there. As I read what I wanted my life to be like, I realized that I had manifested where I am sitting today, almost down to the word.

How did I do this? By starting. I made lists of what I wanted to change and then I DID THE WORK. Let's take my home for example. I was stressed out by the amount of stuff we had that was never used. My space has a big effect on my mood. If things are messy or dirty, I can't think straight. I wanted to make a lot of changes to the house and most required minimal to zero budget. So I went around, room by room and made a list of everything that I didn't like in each room, from wall colour to décor to overstuffed drawers. Everything. I wrote it all down, in the most descriptive detail. Then I brainstormed what I wanted my house to feel like, room by room. I wanted calm, zen, low lighting, good smells. I wanted to take a deep exhale every time I walked in the front door. I wanted to reduce the amount of stuff in the house by at least half. Then, I got to work. I concentrated on one room at a time, going through drawers and emptying shelves. I took car load after car load of donations to the thrift store and dumpster. My life was overwhelming and many parts were out of my control, but the state of my home wasn't. I could take that back. And I did.

I remember when I first posted something about Thomas' special needs getting comments like, "Well if Mare can do all she does and have this going on at home, then I have no excuse." That's right. You have no excuse. You may be reading this on your lowest of lows. You've hit rock bottom and you can't imagine ever pulling yourself up. You may be reading this as the caregiver of someone who is sick, suffering or suicidal. I get those messages all the time. I have been there and I am here on the other side to tell you that anything is possible.

ANYTHING.

Only you can take control of your life. That's it. No one else is going to lose the weight or leave the abusive partner or get a new job. No one else. Only you can. So what the hell are you waiting for?

DO SOME SHIT.

Make the lists. Make the plan. Schedule out what you need to do. Don't let anything get in your way. Then get at doing the work. Your cape thrives on achievement and with every promise you keep to yourself, the cape's strength builds. You say you're going to go hit your step goal five days a week and you actually do it. The cape feels that. You go out for dinner and order a salad instead of fries. The cape perks up. You clean out your closet, a task you've been putting off for months. The cape encourages the self-high five. Your cape wants you to succeed and is there, celebrating every step in the right direction.

One of the biggest roadblocks people stall with is finances. As a single mom, do I ever get this. But if you're serious about your goals, you'll find a way. Can't afford a gym membership? Go for a walk. Go for a run. Watch the zillions of free workout videos on YouTube. Stop buying takeout coffee, stop going out for meals, stop mindless shopping. Once I had specific goals, I truly lost the love of shopping for the sake of the high. I wanted to have a calmer home with less clutter. Now every time I am browsing a store or online shop, I am thinking, "Where can I put this? How will I wear this? Do I have something similar in my closet?" I don't spend nearly as much and my bank account thanks me.

Another excuse is time. Again, where do you think I find the time? The majority of this book was written once Thomas went to bed at night or during his therapist-led Autism appointments, while I hid in another room, typing away on my laptop. I often do client work in my car in between appointments while I quickly eat my lunch. If you want it badly enough, you'll find the time. Carve out the minutes like an appointment. Make a promise to yourself and don't back out or let yourself down. If you struggle with keeping promises to yourself, dig deep and look at why you aren't making progress. Do you have a clear goal in mind? Does your goal need to shift because of new circumstances? Do you need to revisit your action plan? Do you need an accountability buddy? If you've set a goal, why do you want it? For example, I used to want to lose weight to look thinner and look better in clothes. But, as it turns out, I think I look pretty great with my curves! So, the goal to lose weight to look better wasn't working for me. But, when I switched my mindset and re-worked my goal, I started to see success. I am now eating healthy and exercising daily to be healthier long-term. Heart disease runs in my family and I want to be around for a long time for Thomas. So, now when I go to a spin class or I order a side of greens instead of fries, I do so with my head held high. I think of clear arteries and seeing Thomas well into adulthood. What's your why? Every time you stumble, remember why you set this goal in the first place and your cape will be right there, cheering you on.

Another justification for a lack of action? "No one could possibly have it as hard as I do." I call bullshit. I quickly learned that so many people were going through what we were and even worse when I started to share our lives online. I instantly felt less alone and made it my mission to make sure that others felt the same. If you feel like no one can relate or help you, reach out. Find someone who can relate, ask them how they dug themselves out of their hole and then GO FOR IT. If there isn't anyone in your town, find a Facebook group or an online forum to chat. I guarantee there are countless people who have walked your journey and they are further out than you, and would love to share their story.

DO SOME NEW SHIT.

If you keep doing the same thing, do not be confused by the same results.

Try your best to catch yourself when you start to complain. It's human nature, but that energy will stick to you. When you start to feel the "woe is me" monsters coming on, stand down and list as many things as you can that you are grateful for, out loud. It's impossible to play the victim when you are standing in gratitude.

By the way, you're not a victim. You are a strong Mareathoner badass with an invisible cape. Tie that glorious cape around your neck, stand up, and DO SOME SHIT.

Are you surrounding yourself with negative people who also play the victim? Are they negative? Are they the first to scoff at any ideas you might have? This can be incredibly hurtful and curb your willingness to step into your own glorious potential. Be mindful of who you're spending your time with and how you spend your time with certain people. Some people aren't going to be supportive, but others are going to want to hold onto your cape and make it flap in the wind as fast as possible because they are so proud of you and want the world to know! If they aren't supportive of your hard work and your big dreams, they don't get to know them. Period. I have people in my life that I share everything with and others I don't. Time and time again they have proved they won't be excited for me or instantly think that my success somehow means their failure. It doesn't feel good. It hurts. Be aware of these feelings and share accordingly.

Find other people who are doing shit, too. I have some of the strongest friends who I admire. None of us are doing the same thing, and our fields may be very different, but we all have one thing in common: we are productive and progressing. We build each other up and cheer each other on. There is just something so special about a friend who cheers louder than me when I hit a milestone or achieve a goal. So special. Find the people in your life who are also driven and want more for themselves. And if they aren't in your life, join us in the Mareathoner Facebook group. We all hang out there and would love to cheer you on and boost your cape.

Be the person who thrives on productivity, making progress and working towards her goals.

The secret behind doing some shit is this: It's progress over perfection, always. Just start. Don't let yourself get so wrapped up in the need for things to be perfect that you screw yourself over and don't even start. How is that self-love? How is that showing your self-worth? Just START. I don't care what you're doing. As long as you are on your way to your goals, you are an ace in my eyes.

Life is short. It's time to make it the awe-inducing trip you deserve.

The choice is yours. Are you going to DO SOME SHIT?

Ahem, Tough-Love Mare will be going back into her cave in my mind now.

Thanks for indulging her.

Finding Your Cape:

Make a list of the things that keep you up at night. These will be the problems you want to solve, areas of your life to improve, goals you have. Anything. Brain dump and write them down. No judging yourself, just be honest. No one else is going to read this, so make it as raw and real as possible. The sooner you can be honest with yourself, the sooner you'll be on your way to the true change you crave.

Now section them into categories to get a better look at them. Mine are often Thomas, career, relationships, health, home, finances, etc.

One by one, make a list of things you want to change and then a list of what you can do. Prioritize where to start. (If need be, go back and read how I broke things down in making changes to my home.) Then make an action plan. Now it's time to do some shit.

Chapter 12:

Starting a Business to Leave the Business

I WORKED AT THE same radio station in our small city for ten years. I was forever trying to improve and propel myself in my broadcast career, but I could only get so far. I was met with opposition from more than one person who would rattle off gems like, "No one stays in a small town to advance their career; they leave to do that," and "You'll never make as much as him, you're only a woman." We felt stuck in our mortgage as real estate dropped and felt moving away would be a waste of money. I started to think of other avenues I could explore without moving.

In fact, I actually never thought I'd return to radio after my maternity leave. I figured it was a good time to make a break and move into another career to propel my professionnal life. But, once Thomas was born and his special needs were revealed, I decided to stay put and enjoy the comfortable routine of the job, as well as the excellent benefits. All of my energy was dedicated to our beautiful boy. I learned to find reprieve at work, loving my co-host and the on-air experience we created. Our listeners brought us endless joy and helped give me a much-needed laugh. But I never stopped thinking about my next step.

The dawn of social media arrived and the radio station started tagging local businesses on Facebook. There were so many business pages that were lackluster, and I thought maybe I could help. I felt my cape ripple. We needed to stay in our small town because of the incredible support for Thomas, but I started to create an idea out of nowhere that this could be my out. My cape had been patiently waiting for me to find a solution, ready to give me the support I would need. I prepared to propel. I had to start small, try it out, and see if it could work. I talked to the owner of a grocery store who I had worked with on the radio, and we agreed to meet about his social media. I drove around the block that morning, sweating through my button down, because I was so nervous to meet with him. I just drove around and around, trying to talk myself down while pumping myself up. We've all been there, right? Cue my cape. I walked in and pitched to him the idea of doing his Facebook pages for three stores for three months, at no charge. Within a couple of weeks, he phoned to ask me, "What will you charge, and can I tell my friends?"

I had never even considered owning my own business. I had no plan, no budget, no idea what I was doing. That first client from the grocery store had to gently explain that I needed to charge tax! That's how clueless I was. I got all my clients by word of mouth and I still have never advertised for business. I just figured it out with hope a-blazin' and my cape ripplin'. I was ready to progress from my morning radio job and this seemed like my best option.

I just started. I just did some shit. Sometimes we spend waaaaaay too much time on planning the plan instead of executing the damn thing. Instead of just starting and seeing what happens. I started my business on the side, while still working full-time at the radio station and pumping out multiple YouTube videos a week.

My side hustle of helping businesses with their social media pages took off, and in less than a year, I gave my notice at the radio station and shocked virtually everyone in my life. Many people said, "But, you're leaving a good-paying job." Also, "Your job is so fun and you're so good at waking me up, how dare you leave?!" What people didn't know was that behind the scenes and the laughs on the mic, I had been so unhappy for so many years. Those closest to me, those who had listened to me lament year after year were like, "Hell yes!" Jeremy's dad, an entrepreneur himself, said, "You can do whatever you put your mind to." And he was right. I watched a couple of YouTube channels of business people who are entrepreneurs. I made it up as I went. I don't even remember being scared. I remember being hopeful and feeling an incredible weight lift, almost immediately. While I still love the friends I worked with and people who helped me shape my career, it was at times a toxic work environment. I didn't fully realize that until I had distanced myself from the building.

Now, I am not at all encouraging you to quit your career and start a business without a plan! But I am including this chapter of my life to show you that if you know you deserve better, nothing can stop you. It took me years of journaling to unpack why I was so unhappy at work, doing a job that I loved and was very good at. I would free-write in my journal day after day, pouring my thoughts onto the pages until it became clear what was important to me moving forward and what I wanted to leave behind.

Once I left the morning show routine of waking up at 4 a.m., I had to make some shifts and set boundaries. This took me a year. For example, being a morning person, I would wake up before dawn and hit the gym. I would be on the treadmill or lifting weights and see emails roll in from clients who also liked to get ahead before the traditional work day began. I would panic, feeling like I had to stop my sets and take care of the email immediately. It took months of me doing this and feeling that anxiety at just the sight of an email to realize that I needed to step up and set boundaries. So, I switched gears. Now, I don't open my emails until after 9 a.m. and ignore after 6 p.m. If I read them out of business hours, I definitely do not send a reply until the time is appropriate. I don't want clients to think I am available every hour of the day. If it's urgent, they'll call. I am not an on-call doctor for crying out loud! How did my clients respond to my setting boundaries for correspondence? No one's ever said anything. Also, many studies, including one from The National Sleep Foundation, have found that we need to be putting technology down at least an hour before we try to fall asleep. The blue light sends a signal to our brain to be more alert and release cortisol, and lessens the production of melatonin, which is needed to fall asleep.

No. One. Has. Ever. Said. Anything. EVER. Never once. EVER.

If anything, they have said, "I should probably do that too."

If you're an entrepreneur, nothing is hard and fast. Also, nine times out of ten, it's not personal. I had a tough time learning this one, but not taking things personally takes a weight off. I also truly believe that what is for you will not pass you. I've had clients move on, and while I still take a moment to feel the blow, I move on, knowing that time has opened up for other opportunities. I truly believe that what is for me will not pass me.

I realize that not everyone reading this owns a business. (Part of me thinks you are the smart ones!) But I do have some tips on how to wrap that cape around your shoulders when it comes to business, entrepreneur or not.

Tips to Engage Your Cape at Work

Know why you're doing the thing: You need to have a very compelling <u>why</u>. This is just for you, not for anyone else's opinions, thank you very much. You'll want to stop yourself a lot, you'll second-guess yourself a lot, you'll work stupid hours a lot. You hate having a boss? You want to sleep in? You want to have fun? None of these are good enough to sustain momentum, especially on the tough days. For example, my why when I leapt with my cape tied tightly and quit my radio job: *I want to work from home to be there for Jeremy and Thomas, flexible in both my time and earnings, mindful of the energy around me and the possibility to up-level my potential. Having my own business will allow me to provide a fruitful future for our family and one day allow Jeremy to quit his job too.*

Have a schedule and stick to it: Forbes Magazine contributor and entrepreneur John Rampton says people who schedule fewer tasks get more done because you are forced to prioritize what's most important. Tedious tasks can be scrapped or condensed. He also recommends leaving some space free in your schedule to not feel like everything is an overwhelming task.

Never once have I blown off work to watch Netflix all day, ever. You totally could. No one would know. No one's holding you accountable, but that's going to catch up with you really quickly. I would be lying to you if I said I didn't work in my bed. I do work in my pyjamas sometimes, watching Netflix. Also, I schedule in things like exercise and lunch dates. You will need to get out of the house (in a timely manner) to like, breathe fresh air and talk to other humans. Treat these as non-negotiable appointments.

Get dressed every day: I have a shower, put on makeup, and pick out an outfit every day—even if it's just leggings and a tunic. It might sound ludacris, but I promise you will feel more productive and in boss mode if you put in effort for your look. (I am in no way implying you must wear jeans at home. I am not a drill sergeant.) This also comes in handy if a client requests a last-minute meeting or you need to run out and do an errand. If you do work in an office, take pride in how you look, not for anyone else but for yourself. You deserve to feel good every day. Choose looks that make your back a little straighter and your chin higher. The cape goes with any look, honey!

Set boundaries: I already talked about setting work hours and boundaries with replying to emails and texts, etc. On another note about replying, it's okay to set boundaries with friends and family, especially during the work day. Sometimes I think people forget that we are actually working when we have a home office. It's okay to not reply right away, in fact it's imperative for productivity. It's also a boundary for me to rarely work after dinner. My office is right beside my bedroom, but that door closes when I go downstairs to start dinner and remains that way until 9 a.m. Set a physical boundary too with your work space. When I first started Redhead Mare Media, my office was in the laundry room in our basement! I'm talking no windows and replying to business inquiries to the hum of the washer. But it was important to not get into the habit of just sitting with my laptop in the kitchen or the bedroom. Not only is it terrible for my posture and back, but I would just stare at the dishes and the laundry, getting distracted too easily!

Don't be afraid to ask questions: In fact, it's good to ask people questions! Don't have an ego about it. If you don't know the answer, it's okay to say, "I don't know the answer." For some reason I am much better at this professionally than I am in my personal life. Remember how great you feel when you get to help someone or offer your expertise. Allow someone else that honour to help you.

The cape is my invisible boost every day in my home office, in a meeting or in a presentation. Heck, if you need to physically mime putting it on in the privacy of your car or a bathroom stall before going into an interview or a pitch, do it! Key point: in *private*. We don't want to scare them off before we even start, do we?

Chapter 13:

You Do You

IMAGINE IF YOU could tally up how much time you've wasted worrying about what others think of you. Wasting time makes my skin crawl, so doing this exercise would make me climb under the covers to hide. It's similar to the annoyance or disgust I feel when I think of how much time I've wasted thinking about certain boys who turned out to be not even worth a follow on Instagram. *facepalm*

If you can relate, don't get down on yourself, it's totally human nature. We all worry about what others think of us. But here's the secret: more often than not, they too are worried about what others think of THEM. We are all absorbed in our own stuff and self-conscious; it's all just a waste of time. I reckon humans could solve global warming, cure cancer, and discover how to find the perfect bra/pair of jeans without stepping foot into a change room, if we stopped wasting our precious minds on the thoughts of others.

Here's where the Mareathoner mantra comes in: **You Do You**. (I truly wish there was a way to insert audible fanfare whenever I write these words. For a second, can you please just hear it in your mind as I say it again?)

You Do You.

I am not exactly sure when You Do You became the mantra of the Mareathon, but it's taken off like wildfire in our community. I started saying it all the time, on the air, to my friends, in videos, and it just stuck. The You Do You sweatshirt was the first piece of clothing I launched and I even got the phrase tattooed on my right forearm to celebrate hitting one million views on YouTube.

I first started saying You Do You at a time in my life when I didn't feel I had much, if any, control or say in how things were unfolding. I constantly felt like I was hanging on for dear life, waiting for the next free-fall. To an outsider, things may have looked perfect. I was on the number one morning radio show locally, raising a beautiful son with a loving husband in an enviable town. According to the online highlight reel, I had it all.

But inside our bubble, the truth was different. Jeremy's mental health had spiralled into suicidal thoughts. Thomas is the love of my life, but after he was diagnosed as hard of hearing at birth and Autistic at three, managing his therapies and services and subsequent paperwork became a full-time job. I felt like I was juggling precious lives in the air, but no one had ever taught me how to juggle. Just when I figured out how to get one ball in the air and floating comfortably, another would threaten to drop. I was not doing me, I was just barely surviving. Even though I knew it wasn't okay, I couldn't comprehend what else to do. I couldn't lift myself out of the mud long enough to even think about how to pull the three of us out of the sinking, heavy reality around us. I slowly but surely took over more responsibilities in our relationship and home as Jeremy worked on stabilizing himself.

I kept saying You Do You as a way for me to subconsciously do just that. This was my cape, propping me up. The cape acted as an invisible shield against the ever-present threat of collapse. It could feel my fragility and consistently gave me strength to persevere. It reminded me of past triumphs, bringing visual reminders that I was strong enough to figure out a way to go on. I could do it because I'd done it before. I was doing what I needed to, in order to keep our family afloat. I didn't need everyone in our lives to agree, we'd do what was best for us. You Do You.

When you make a decision that is not true to your core values, your body tells you. Instantly. For me, my body and breath react. I feel a contraction in my stomach and legs, shortness of breath and quickening of my heartbeat. The same happens when I am not living by You Do You.

So what exactly does this mantra mean?

You Do You is a mantra for living your authentic self. You are making decisions based on your inner voice and core values. Ever say yes to something you absolutely do not want to? Or turn down an opportunity because it scares you? Ever laugh awkwardly at someone's joke you actually find offensive? That twinge you get in your stomach is your soul's way of saying "HELLO?!? This is NOT what we want or what we stand for!" You can ignore her, suppress what you want for the sake of others, and live how you think your family, coworkers, or friends expect you to behave. Continuing doing all of this, but that inner voice will not go away. It is a superhero who cannot be denied, always at the ready. The more you act in a way that is not your authentic self, the worse you will feel.

Think of the cape as a symbol of your inner voice.

The Many Colours of You Do You (not limited to, but including):

- ★ Owning your weirdness
- ★ Finding yourself and then actually being yourself
- ★ Standing firm in your beliefs
- ★ Standing up for others and for yourself
- ★ Being considerate of others
- ★ Doing what feels good to you, regardless of what others think
- ★ Making choices because it's what your gut is telling you
- ★ Delaying a decision to get quiet and listen to your inner voice
- ★ Politely turning away from other people's opinions
- ★ Knowing the difference between being alone and being lonely
- ★ Letting go of resentment—both towards others and towards yourself
- ★ Politely ignoring the expectations of others
- ★ Taking the time to take care of yourself, really and truly
- ★ Recognizing when someone is toxic and giving yourself permission to walk away
- ★ Putting your needs first
- ★ Protecting yourself from negative and poisonous people

Living by You Do You takes courage. Real, visceral, dig--down-deep courage. Sweaty courage. Saying-no-to-things courage. Saying-yes-to-things courage. Want-to-throw-up--your-lunch courage. I hope you are starting to understand why we need that magical cape. Mine has the mantra flowing between its threads.

The only caveat to this mantra is that this behaviour doesn't purposely hurt anyone else. I hope we all get that and it goes without saying, but here I am, saying it, just for good measure.

The people who are most uncomfortable with this mantra are the ones who are too scared to live it themselves. It will mean that you have to respectfully disagree with someone's opinion. Over and over and over again. And if they won't show you respect in return, you may need to find new people. I've known people (I bet you have, too) whose own self-esteem is so low that they need everyone to agree with them to the point of bullying. We don't all have to agree. In fact, can we please not? Life would be so boring if we all agreed! It's healthy to disagree, to go different ways, and to do different things. We need all types of people in this world and we need them to march to their own beat.

You do not have to apologize for doing what sets your heart on fire. My dad died when he was 57 and Jeremy at 35. This taught me that *life is short*. We are only here for a finite amount of time, so why are we not running towards the things that make us happy?! I have become much more pro-active in making memories. I've had pushback from people who think I shouldn't be sharing my story and say I am just trying to make a quick buck. But I know in my soul that I have a purpose and obligation to share what I have learned to help you make better choices. A huge and courageous aspect of You Do You is knowing that other people's negative and ignorant opinions bear no weight. In fact, these opinions usually have nothing to do with you, but instead their fears and insecurities are projecting onto you.

You Do You. Without apology.

There is another side to this: allowing others the grace of You Do You. Admittedly, I have to work at recognizing when others need to live by the mantra. When I think someone's behaviour is making their life more difficult, or I can see how things could improve and up-level and they refuse to take action, I have to consciously step back. If it is not appropriate to offer advice, I need to let it go. There's a saying that what you find most annoying about someone else is often a reflection of what bothers you about yourself. I will admit that, for me, that trait would involve being judgmental. I unknowingly clench my teeth and tighten my stomach when I feel judged, but I definitely do it to others. A huge part of You Do You is giving space for others to do what they see as best for themselves.

You cannot control anyone, and you cannot force them to change. My dad was obese and struggled with his weight most of his life. I never understood why my mum didn't force him to take care of himself. She always said, "You cannot force someone to change, Marianne, they have to want to do it themselves." (This also goes out to anyone who is in a relationship and thinks they can just change their partner.) The effort becomes a waste of energy and can project things onto them. I try to lead by example. If someone's behaviour continues to bother me, it may be time to consider stepping back and analyzing the relationship and my own insecurities.

The You Do You mantra allows you the life you deserve, making the choices that will make you happy. It also helps let go of judgement and support others as they live their best lives. I am not saying that you can't gently offer help or suggestions to work as a community with your tribe. But if someone is hell-bent on self-sabotage, it is not your place to take control or your problem to fix. Take that energy you've been wasting worrying what others think or judging and transfer it to creating the life YOU want. How could you ever begin to create the life you deserve, the one that makes you leap out of bed in the morning and collapse back on the mattress at night with a satisfied smile, if you are too busy thinking about everyone else's opinions?

It's crucial to listen to that cape and then once you can hear it, to give it the strength to show you what steps to take.

Now, put on that cape and get to living by You Do You.

Finding Your Cape:

★ Write about times in your life in which you haven't lived by You Do You.
★ Why did you do that?
★ Whose opinions are you putting ahead of your own?
★ What are you not doing because you are worried what other people will think?
★ How did that make you feel?
★ In what ways have you lived by You Do You?
★ How do you feel when you do live by the mantra?
★ Brainstorm inspirational examples of others living by You Do You.

Chapter 14:

Anger: The A-Hole of A-Words

NGER IS KIND of a foreign concept to me. Now, before you roll your eyes at this redheaded Leo and call BS that I am happy all the time, let me explain.

Anger is not something I grew up with. That probably sounds dramatic, but it's the truth. I have never heard my mum raise her voice even once. My dad had a quiet calmness about him. He was never angry, but would share his "I am disappointed in you" looks instead. I never saw my parents disagree. Not once. They were always a united front. I assume they had disagreements in private after I'd gone to bed or when I was out of earshot, but it was never for me to witness.

So when I am asked why I don't share my anger online, it's because I just don't share it at all. Period. Wow. I actually didn't realize that until I wrote those words just now. I don't even share the full extent of my anger with myself. Sure I get upset or mad, but it's usually pretty fleeting. I just don't see the point. I don't like to dwell on the negative, preferring to find a solution quickly and move on. Why have I never shared my anger with my online community? It's never even occurred to me to put that out into the world. There is already so much hate and unrest, why add to it? I have mentioned it in fleeting comments, but nothing substantial.

I recognize this is not healthy and not the norm. In marriage counselling, my therapist would teach me that anger was necessary, and a healthy way to disagree. It's always made me super uncomfortable. If Jeremy raised his voice, it would instantly throw me into a fit of tears, feeling like I was going to throw up. He wanted to be able to get out his frustration and I would bottle mine up, further and further away.

I struggle with sharing aspects of my anger because I feel real shame embedded in this emotion, especially when it comes to talking about being a widow. I can be one hell of an angry widow at times, don't get me wrong. But, it seems politically incorrect and insensitive to talk about my anger because outsiders would say Jeremy was the one who suffered, the one who was suicidal. Jeremy was the one who took his own life at the age of 35. But, after all of that, what about the ones who are left? (Even writing these words and including this in the book is out of my comfort zone, but I've got the cape on, knowing this is important.)

Anger.

Dr. Cynthia Thaik, Harvard-trained holistic cardiologist, says that anger can manifest itself in the body in a myriad of terrifying ways such as high blood pressure, anxiety, headaches, restricted circulation and more. Research shows that even five minutes of anger can impair your immune system for more than six hours.

It wasn't until I started writing this book that I realized I was hiding this aspect of my journey. My editor Simone revealed that after one of our very first sessions she walked away with a new sense of my anger and, as a Mareathoner herself, she'd never seen that side or heard me talk of it. Ever.

So here we go.

"Aren't you mad at Jeremy?" Hell yes I am angry. One of the things I have struggled with the most in my grief after Jeremy's suicide is anger.

Well, backing up, there was a lot of anger before that too: Angry that Thomas has been dealt a special needs hand. Angry that we can't have a "normal" life together with birthday parties and soccer teams and playdates. Angry that sometimes nothing I try helps Thomas.

Angry that Jeremy's mental health had such a rapid downward spiral. Angry that nothing he tried worked. Angry that we didn't have more family support in town. Angry that everything seemed to be my job and responsibility. Angry that Jeremy couldn't seem to make friends and have a healthy social life. Angry that I let him make me feel guilty for having one.

Angry that I don't have the perfect body. Angry that I can work incredibly hard on my diet and exercise and still be overweight.

Angry that people seemed to easily take and take from me, giving nothing in return.

Angry that my dad didn't take good enough care of his health and he died when I was 19.

Angry that... Yeah, now that you ask, there's a lot of anger inside of me.

Anger is a common part of grief and, let me tell you, I've got a lot of it. How could he leave his boy without a dad? How could he leave his special needs son, who has already been dealt so many blows in his short life, without a dad? As I write this, Thomas is nearing the end of grade two, and every day I gently pull him down the street as he looks over his shoulder with eager anticipation, looking for his dad. Every day I wonder, "How the hell could you do this to your son?"

Anger comes in waves as I grieve. Well, maybe it's always there, underlying and waiting to surge, but rarely rears its ugly head. In the first few months I'd frequently have moments of blinding anger, unable to breath or think or function. It would literally bring me to my knees in despair. These spells still happen, once in a while. But that's the thing about anger... what is the point? What do you do next?

I'd been so tightly wound, holding on to every uncomfortable emotion during Jeremy's last two years. To give you an idea of just how tight I was, shortly after his funeral I started meditating and I couldn't even take one deep breath. Not one. My chest had been tight and restricted in panic for so long that I couldn't even enjoy a deep cleansing inhale. I was too constricted to relax. The complex whirling of emotions from caregiver to widow created an unimaginable weight that pulled up a seat on my chest and wouldn't budge.

Now I recognize that bottling everything up is not the route to take. A part of me does wish I had been shown how to convey anger in a constructive way and work through the feelings as a child. It's much better to be honest with the people in your life and tell them when you're hurting. That being said, I am incredibly grateful that my parents showed me how useless it is to hold on to anger.

You must find a balance. Grasp the cape around your shoulders and allow it to help you process the anger. Your cape can help you breathe through the emotions, patiently waiting as you consider why you feel the way you do. For example, if I am angry, most of the time that's not the real root of the issue. I am late to take Thomas to school (again) and I cannot pick out something to wear. Nothing looks right, fits or makes me feel good. A full closet of clothes and nothing to wear. I spiral in my mind with angry thoughts of, "Why don't you exercise more?" and "You're so lazy" and "Why are you always rushed in the morning? You should be faster." This can go round and round, when really I am angry because I am tired and trying to do too many things at once. So I pause, visualize the cape, and turn my inner dialogue to a more loving commentary. When you catch yourself in a sinkhole of negative self-talk, think, "Would I say this to a friend?" Start talking to yourself like you would your best friend. Because, you ARE your best friend.

If it's not dealt with properly, anger will manifest in ugly ways like physical pain or lashing out at an unsuspecting bystander. Often parents in my online community will admit to unexpectedly taking their anger out on their spouse or child. This is not okay and can be avoided. Take a self-imposed time out. If you're finding yourself in an escalating situation with someone (or your own self-talk), stop and walk away, with your cape securely fastened. You are entitled to take the time to process how you are feeling before circling back to the conversation. Don't let someone pressure you into continuing to lash out. I have found myself angry without being able to quickly pinpoint why. So I excuse myself and take the steps to figure it out. Then I come back and can succinctly explain.

Put on the Cape and Start Processing Anger in a Productive Way:

Let it out: Find someone who is in your tribe who will listen. It's good to get it out and to have a sounding board. Often they will have been through the same thing or know someone who has. Problems get blown way out of proportion when you keep them to yourself. Look for someone who will first listen without jumping into fix-it mode. Often we just need to speak the anger out loud to hear how silly it sounds and the energy dissipates. For this portion, again, I cannot recommend enough finding a good therapist. Mine have changed my life. You do not have to reinvent the wheel. Allow them to impart their experience and tools to deal with your anger.

Marian Margulies, PhD, a psychologist in New York City and candidate in psychoanalysis at the Institute for Psychoanalytic Education at the NYU Medical Center, noted in a Forbes Magazine interview that therapy can actually change the brain. She says with brain imaging methods, psychotherapy has been shown to alter activity in the areas of the brain involved in thoughts such as worrying, emotion, and fear.

Talk it out: Surround yourself with people who value your opinion and want you to speak up for yourself. It's beneficial to have a couple of people in your circle who can act as a sounding board when you find yourself in an awkward situation. Instead of going round and round in your own mind, they can help you talk it out in a safe space. Once you have let it out, get set to talk it out with the person who has made you feel angry. Time and time again, I am struck by how easily a conversation goes when I am direct and honest about my feelings.

Write it out: Whether it's a note on your phone, a document on your computer or a journal: WRITE. Writing has given me so much clarity over the years. I brain dump, just writing without judgment, re-reading, or thinking. It's amazing how you can come to simple conclusions or solutions within the pages of a journal. Often I find that I can just let something go by writing it out.

Sweat it out: The Anxiety and Depression Association of America says because stress affects the brain, it can be felt throughout the body. So, if you move your body and it feels better, your mind will follow suit. The ADAA says exercise is also good to improve your sleep, which in turn, reduces stress and anger. Scientists say even five minutes of aerobic exercise can stimulate anti-anxiety effects.

Find a way to get your heart pumping at least three times a week—my go-tos have become a high-level flow yoga class or a spin session. I like that in both exercise classes, there is no way I can think of anything except the exact task at hand. I can't dwell on the last song or pose because I'm currently trying to not fall out of the current one. I also love throwing on my headphones and going for a long, brisk walk. Something about fresh air settles my mind.

One last note about anger. Putting on the cape to sensitively deal with your anger is the end goal. We do not don our cape to give us strength to lash out or bring others down in anger. This is not the Mareathoner way. Find the balance of expressing yourself with intention. Anger is a healthy and important emotion, something to be felt, expressed, processed, and then released.

Allow yourself to feel the feels with this particular a-word. Allow the cape to carry you. Allow yourself grace in letting it go.

Chapter 15:

The Unwanted Houseguest

T HE OTHER A-WORD, not to be mistaken for an a-hole, is anxiety.

Anxiety is like the unwanted houseguest who shows up unannounced and stays even though she is NOT welcome. The more you try to ignore her and power through, whisking around the house pretending she isn't there, the more she makes a mess. She gets angry, wants attention, and throws a hissy fit. My therapist gave me a helpful tip and recommended I picture my anxiety as a shape, sitting in my body, wherever I felt it taking up space. (I feel anxiety in my stomach.) So I started to say, "Oh hey anxiety, you're back again. I feel you there in my stomach, but I will not interact. You can stay here, but know you aren't welcome and I will not collaborate with you. It's better if you just quietly let yourself out when you're ready to leave." The more I tried to power through and overcome the anxiety, the harder it would fight back. But, if I made space and allowed her to set up in my stomach, every time she'd slip away without me realizing.

I started to experience full-blown anxiety for the first time in my life soon after Jeremy became suicidal. I was spent emotionally and physically. I hadn't even dealt with or come to terms with the trauma of Thomas' multiple diagnoses, the months of emergency room visits, appointments, and constant terror. Now I was thrown into a new, terrifying scenario, barely catching my breath. I scored so high on the depression/anxiety testing, that my doctor put me on medication.

It was bad and I knew it. I wasn't taking care of myself, but again, as the caregiver for both Jeremy and Thomas, I didn't know how to make the time for that. Instead of taking care of myself, I started going out with friends on the weekend, drinking and using that as an escape. The alcohol didn't numb my pain. It amplified it. Many people think alcohol helps to quiet the mind, but in fact, it is a depressant. I cried every day. No exaggeration. Every. Single. Day. In the shower, the car, at work, at the gym, out for a walk. I cried myself to sleep every night. My aunt was genuinely concerned that I was barreling toward a nervous breakdown.

The meds did nothing. Deep down I knew I didn't actually need pills. I needed to make major changes. I believe many people DO need medication to help the chemical imbalance that cause mental health issues. I know many people who have seen their lives improve exponentially on medication. Talk to your doctor if you're struggling and they will be able to guide you in the right direction. But for me, I'd neglected myself long enough. It was time to do some shit.

My cape had been patiently waiting for me to call upon it. When we are making decisions that are not in our best interest, we know we are ignoring our cape and our inner voice. It was time for me to pull on the cape again and get to work. The cape held my past strength in overcoming tough times and I would need it more than ever this time. Here's what I did to combat this hella unwelcome anxiety:

I went to therapy. Every week. For four years. I still do check-ins when necessary. (In fact I've seen my therapist a few times in writing this book, hey girl!)

I journaled like my life depended on it. Because it did. Sometimes I would journal thirty pages in one sitting, filling notebook after notebook.

I stopped eating meat. I was sick of feeling uncomfortable all the time. This is not for everyone, but I suggest you look at what you're eating and how it makes you feel. Maybe a plant--based diet isn't for you, but you do deserve to be mindful of what you eat and how it makes you feel.

I gave up coffee. I know. Unimaginable! Caffeine amped up my anxiety, made my heart race and my hands shake.

I stopped drinking. I quickly learned that getting a buzz doesn't make your problems go away, it brings them to the forefront of your mind while your defences are dulled.

I physically removed myself from my space, taking a trip to see a friend who lives two provinces away. She worked all day and I sat in her house in the dead of a Saskatchewan winter... more journaling. Removing yourself from your everyday space can give you clarity and time to breathe.

I quit my job. I realize this is not practical for everyone. But I had built my side hustle business to a point where I was ready. I just needed a push. So I pushed MYSELF.

I started meditating and doing yoga. Not regularly, but I started to recognize the value in being present. According to my favourite meditation app, Headspace, there are thousands of studies that have shown that mindfulness meditation can positively impact mental and physical health. Mindfulness works, and that is backed by science. A study conducted by researchers at the University of Oxford found eight weeks of Headspace reduced symptoms of anxiety in employees. Research shows that mindfulness training can improve the quality of sleep for individuals with sleeping difficulties.

I walked. I've always found walking with loud music gives me an outlet to expel energy, think and get some fresh air.

I found my cape. I realized I can only save myself. I started to really lean into my cape to give me strength like a superhero. I felt I was fighting a battle and drew strength in the belief that this was not my future. This was not how I was meant to live my life. Quietly I tied the cape around my shoulders, and little by little, I felt its courage. I started making incredibly difficult decisions and implementing new habits. This by no means kicked my anxiety to the curb, but it definitely helped prevent it from coming through the proverbial door of my house. I kept her on the stoop, quietly sitting in my stomach until she stopped showing up as much.

But then Jeremy took his life and my anxiety was back. I would get a wave of anxious energy every morning at precisely 7:40. Like a jolt, anxiety would blast in and angrily stomp around. This lasted for months and I allowed her to work out her anger in my stomach, getting used to my new reality as a widow and single parent. I knew that fighting the anxiety just makes it worse, so I would breathe and do what I could until it passed.

It's no mystery why this a-word stomped in every morning at the exact same time. Jeremy used to be responsible for Thomas' morning routine. I would wake up at about 5:30 and head straight into my office to work while Jer got Thomas fed, bathed and ready for school. He took him to school. In a split second, this all became my responsibility along with everything else, and anxiety used that to make a lot of noise in my world.

Anxiety will still show up now and then, but I can instantly recognize her and show her the door. It no longer upsets me because I know that's a cycle that will pass: you are anxious that you feel anxiety, you get upset and then you are annoyed that you are upset. It's a vortex of emotion that no one signs up for.

When anxiety does pop in, I encourage you to gently consider its trigger. Have you taken on too much? Are you feeling resentful? Are you anticipating something? When I first felt anxious, the triggers were obvious and seemingly unavoidable. But now I have curated a life that is much healthier and calmer, so anxiety is an outsider. I'm getting better at recognizing this, but like anything else, it's a process.

I've witnessed anxiety at its absolute worst in Jeremy. I didn't understand it for a long time and honestly, sometimes it was difficult to support him. True, crippling anxiety is virtually impossible to understand if you've never experienced it. Why can't they just snap out of it and get over it? Move on? Man up? But would you tell someone with a broken leg to just get up and walk, pretending like nothing was wrong? Would you tell someone fighting cancer to get over it? No, you wouldn't. Mental health is just the same. It actually gets worse the more you ignore it AND the more you fuel it. It's also different in everyone.

Jeremy was an instrumental barrier-breaker in the mental health fight, sharing his story and publicly inspiring hundreds of people to get help themselves. There is no doubt in my mind he's saved so many lives. His decision to be honest and vulnerable in a very public way, has given so many people the courage to get help. I continue to get messages from people all over the world telling me how his advice is in the forefront of their mind.

Finding Your Cape:

Recognize what your triggers for anxiety are and brainstorm how you can reduce or eliminate them. If you can't, how can you at least be prepared for them?

Visualize your anxiety, locate where you feel it in your body and give it a name. Be prepared to give it a little speech the next time it shows up. Mine is, "Hello there Anxiety. I feel you, but I will not engage with you. You are toxic and unwelcome, but I will not force you off my front stoop. I will not give you power by trying to fight you."

Think of changes you can make to your day, home or work environment that will ease your anxiety triggers. Don't worry, through all of this, the cape is with you.

Chapter 16:

You Can Do Anything for Ten Minutes

I MAGINE IF WE could tally and keep track of how many thoughts we had in one day. Heck, even one hour. I would bet money it's in the tens of thousands. Every second your mind can flit from thought to thought. Here's an accurate depiction of my mind this morning:

"Am I anxious? Does this romper make me look fat? Do I care if it does? I love my body. How would I ever get rid of this cellulite? I spend too much time on my phone. Will I ever meet someone? How am I going to meet him? These online dating apps are useless. Why did I not get enough done yesterday? Wait, I did a lot—stop being so unkind to yourself. You're amazing! I guess I'll make Thomas dinner before I go to yoga. Don't forget to get gas. I hope his dentist appointment goes okay today. I can't wait for lunch. Can I nap today? How am I ever going to feel rested? I wonder what's happening on Instagram today..."

Aren't you exhausted just reading that? Surely that's not even the full scope of it; I am forgetting the thoughts in between those ones, judging my thoughts, questioning everything, and then moving on to the next.

Breathe. The only way out is through, and we are going through this together. Tie on that cape and get ready to get courageous. In this chapter I want to talk about being mindful. Everywhere we turn lately that seems to be a buzz-word, but to me it's one of the single most life-altering practices.

Basically, being mindful means that you work on consistently bringing yourself back to the present. Over and over and over again. Then when you can't do it anymore, you do it again. You're going to need to visualize that cape because being present is one of the most courageous, daily practices I recommend. You cape deserves a moment to rest and be present, we all do. The cape will quietly wait and be recharged right along with you as you bring yourself back to the present.

I have spent years of my life not being present. I was so worried about what was about to happen or what could happen. For so long I was just treading water, trying to take good care of Thomas while being there for Jeremy, taking as much off of his plate as possible as he worked on his mental health. I was in survival mode—just trying to get through one hellish day after another, while dreaming of a simpler and happier time. Being present was often too painful and confusing, and I'd quickly busy myself to think of anything else. Distraction became a way to numb. Friends would genuinely ask how I was and I'd consistently divert the conversation back to asking about them instead. Don't make me focus on my pain, let's talk about yours instead!

Here are a few examples of ways we numb via distraction:
- ★ gossip
- ★ keeping busy with a tightly booked calendar
- ★ taking care of others

★ mindlessly scrolling social media
★ pinning endless ideas on Pinterest boards we will never explore
★ gaming, whether on your phone or computer or television
★ eating
★ drinking alcohol
★ using drugs
★ working on unnecessary projects
★ shopping online or in store
★ bingeing a television series
★ obsessively exercising to the point of exhaustion or hurting yourself

Some of these may surprise you. I used to think that being busy was a badge of honour. I loved to constantly have a show or YouTube video on in the background, no matter what I was doing. I thought I was multitasking and slaying the day. Then I realized that I was busy because I was avoiding being present or listening to my own thoughts. I couldn't possibly deal with overwhelming emotions and issues if I was helping someone else or hitting play on yet another episode of my current television series obsession. It took being forced into my worst nightmare to get me to be mindful and present.

Some of my memory is blurred by absolute terror and numbed in pain when I try to recall specifics around his death. But one thing that is crystal clear is the advice a friend gave me as I prepared to meet with the funeral home for the first time. "You can do anything for ten minutes." Anything for ten minutes. Another friend would whisper this to me as I was introduced at Jeremy's funeral for the eulogy. And again months later as we laid him to rest.

You can do anything for ten minutes.

These seven words bring me calm, strength, and the ability to persevere.

In an instant, this changed my mindset. I *can* do anything for ten minutes. It made it much less daunting when I would focus on just one ten-minute chunk. Then on the next. Then the next. And so on. I repeated her advice constantly in the coming weeks and months.

You can do anything for ten minutes.

This was the unintentional beginning of my mindset shift to focusing on the present.

I started making each decision as a new widow thoughtfully and with intention, before moving on to the next. Of course I was overwhelmed to say the least, but looking at things in ten-minute increments helped me focus and block out the rest of the noise. I use this technique in spin class, telling myself to just get through the song playing. I use it on tired days when I am overwhelmed by responsibilities, breaking the day into one task at a time. I use it during hard conversations, focusing on exactly what is happening without overanalyzing or thinking ahead.

Being present is a constant work-in-progress for me. It's a daily practice of catching thoughts and bringing myself back to the present moment. Every. Single. Day. It's also crucial to catch yourself in thoughts and bring yourself back to the present *without judging yourself.*

Tools That Help My Mindset:

Deep Breaths: Never question the healing power of a few deep, focused breaths. When I start to feel overwhelmed or scattered, I immediately return to my breath and check in. It became a goal to work through my grief to get back to the point where I could take a glorious deep breath. Just a few deep breaths will steady my pulse and bring me back to the present. Here's a couple things I like to do when taking some deep, cleansing breaths. I consciously think, "inhale lightness, exhale tightness," and picture my body becoming lighter and less restricted. Another thing that helps is to choose colours to focus on. For example, I picture a beautiful pale pink colour entering my body as I inhale, representing health and lightness and calm. When I exhale, I picture my body sending out a murky black, letting go of any negativity. Some people like to count as they breathe. A common practice is counting in for four, hold for four, exhale for four, hold for four. I know nervous flyers who find this to be incredibly helpful. Focusing on your breath forces you to be present and to think of nothing else but how lucky you are to be able to take those deep breaths, never taking that simple ability for granted.

Meditation: According to the National Center for Complementary and Integrative Health, some research suggests that meditation may physically change the brain and body and could potentially help to improve many health problems and promote healthy behaviors.

At first, I brushed meditation off as something hippy dippy that I most certainly did NOT have time for. Also, who on Earth wants to sit quietly with their thoughts? NO thank you!

But, I was desperate to try anything for clarity and comfort. I needed to slow the relentless noise in my head of thoughts going around and around. I dabbled and found it helped. I even got up at 3:45 a.m. each day, so I could light a candle and meditate for fifteen minutes before heading to my morning radio show job. I used a free guided meditation from a colleague. It didn't stick then, but I began a daily meditation ritual just a couple of weeks after Jeremy's death. At this point, I had to find something to bring me back to the present; I felt my mind was whirling out of control. Meditation has taught me so much about myself, about the way I think, and allowed me to hear that inner voice. I know we often want to squash that inner critic and blast anything and everything to drown it out, but it doesn't go away. Giving it space to be heard is powerful. Meditation brings you to the present in just a few deep breaths. Also, you don't have to call it meditation. Call it whatever makes you comfortable. Use a guided segment if you like or just sit quietly and breathe. Notice your thoughts, acknowledge them and then gently bring your concentration back to your breath. You're never going to quiet your mind completely, this is not the goal. The goal is to slow things down and come back to the present, listening to your breath. Over and over.

I like guided meditations so I use the Headspace app. I like how easy it is to navigate. I open the app and my next meditation is right there, waiting to start. I find the narrator's voice very calming. I do the ten minute meditations; again, you can do anything for ten minutes. If Headspace isn't for you, there are many different apps and options. YouTube has countless free guided meditations. I have found meditation to be the best way to make tough decisions, as it quiets the rest of the noise and allows me clarity.

Again, the cape is partly a symbol for your inner voice. Quiet everything else to allow yourself to truly hear the cape and let it take a breather as well. I like to meditate first thing in the morning. This sets me up for a calmer, more present day. Meditating at night will also help relax your brain and lull you to sleep. I've meditated sitting in my car on a stressful day, in the booth at the radio station, on a train, a plane, you name it.

Not every meditation is zen or perfect. Some days are much more challenging, but stick with it. Work to get to a place where you welcome your thoughts and want to sit in silence to hear them.

Mindful Scrolling: I love social media. I love it so much I've built a business around it! But, an easy way to get lost in the past or the future or in the comparison game is to mindlessly scroll. Remind yourself that social media is, for the most part, not real life. Catch yourself scrolling and check in to see how you feel. I have days where I can physically feel my mood and self-worth plummeting with every tap of my thumb. Check in with who you're following on social media. A good test I like to do when I scroll Instagram is to be aware of how I feel with every photo or story I pass. If I don't want to double tap, I pause and ask myself why. I have unfollowed hundreds of accounts, some because they are negative and trashy, but others because they are obviously just a highlight reel. I want authenticity and reality in my social media. I have met countless Mareathoners who crave the same thing. I love to scroll social media, but making sure it is intentional and mindful, the experience is healthier, purposeful. Your social media feed is *yours*. Own it, protect it, cherish it.

Time Management: This is a great follow-up to mindless scrolling. I recommend you track how you spend your time for two days and see how often you aren't present. Many phones now have a screen time monitor and I encourage you to face reality by tracking how much time you're on your phone. It will even tell you how many times you pick it up in an hour. How does that number make you feel? Remember, it might feel numbing and therefore "great" in the moment, but really analyze your mental state. When I heard that it takes 15 minutes to check your social media and then get back on track, I realized just how much time I was wasting. I came up with so much extra time every day once I was strict with time management. I often get asked how I manage to do so much being a single parent running a business. Time management, baby!

Track your day and see how you are spending your time. Then, look at how you can consolidate your tasks or batch them. Take cooking for example: I found that making Thomas' school lunch in the morning would stress me out, so instead, I always put together his lunch the night before as I make dinner. I am in the kitchen anyway, and now barely notice that it's an extra task. Same goes for making my own food. I used to meal plan for the whole week and grocery shop on Sundays. This meant no guesswork during the busy work week and we always had delicious, nutritious food. As a single mum, I beat myself up when I couldn't handle this anymore. I didn't want to plan meals, and cooking for just Thomas and I felt insurmountable. Suddenly *everything* was my responsibility, and something had to give. So I now have a few go-to meals that give me a ton of leftovers but are quick to make. I always have a big green salad in the fridge with various toppings like quinoa, tofu, nuts, pickles, etc. This way

I can easily make a delicious and nutritious meal in no time at all. I'll spend an extra few minutes one day prepping the salad, and then I don't have to think about it. Instead of overthinking what I will make for dinner every night, I can be present with my other tasks.

Time management also means encouraging your brain to be present when you are around others. Put the phone away or on silent and engage with who is physically in front of you. Focus on the current conversation; those notifications will still be there when you're ready to check them, and the person who you're spending time with will know you value them.

Journaling: We often find our minds are going so quickly that we can't keep up. It races and spirals and we create all kinds of nonsensical stories. Journaling helps with this immensely. I journaled and brain dumped so much during the worst years with Jeremy that I easily filled notebook after notebook. Even when I was writing it out years ago, I remember thinking: "You'll want to reflect and see how far you've come one day." The quality of my penmanship directly reflects the intensity of the day. So many pages are virtually illegible and that's completely fine. The purpose of getting your thoughts on to paper isn't to go back and analyze. It is to get your thoughts out to free up brain space and quiet that noise. You can only think as fast as you write, so you're forced to slow down to one thought at a time. I highly recommend you use an actual notebook and pen to engage in the physical act of writing. If you don't like writing in a journal, try typing a note in your phone or using a voice memo. You could even film yourself just to get it out.

Being Grateful, Out Loud: If you only do one of these, do this. Every day. Start with gratitude and I promise you that things will slowly come into focus. Nothing brings me to this exact present moment more than making a list, out loud, of the things I am grateful for. Try it. Right now. Let me hear it.

Some days you will feel like you have nothing to list, but that's just not true. Here's a perfect example of my gratitude list on a really low day, soon after Jeremy passed away:

I am grateful because:

- ★ I can breathe
- ★ I can walk
- ★ I can hear
- ★ I can talk
- ★ I am safe
- ★ I am loved
- ★ Thomas
- ★ I have a reliable car
- ★ I have a business that affords me food and a home
- ★ I love my home
- ★ I am supported
- ★ I made it through another day

See? You don't have to come up with some all-powerful, meaningful, grandiose list. I find the simpler the list, the more gratitude I feel. I mean, how can I continue to be stressed about work when I realize how lucky I am to be able to walk, breathe, hear, etc.? I often list, out-loud, ten things I am grateful for as I drive. This is also a powerful exercise to do at night instead of running through everything that went terribly that day or focusing on what you didn't do. Some keep a gratitude journal or a list in their phone. This can be helpful to reference, especially on particularly low days. Gratitude is the ultimate mindset shift.

Remember: you are not your thoughts. Get in the habit of physically picturing your negative thoughts bouncing off your cape onto the ground and rolling away from you. Being aware of your thoughts and realizing that you can change them is incredibly powerful. Again, cue that billowing cape. The more you are able to be present, the more the cape will take those negative thoughts and let them go.

No one can make you think a certain way. You control whether you're agonizing over the past, resenting someone or thinking negatively about the future.

You. And only you.

When you focus on the present moment things are simpler. More focused. You'll enjoy so much more of every day when you are present. Mindfulness dissipates daily pressure and brings you to the present. Pressure vs present. To be mindful is a daily practice, and remember, you can do anything for ten minutes.

Finding Your Cape:

Make notes throughout the day of how often you find yourself not being present and then ways in which you could flip this mindset.

Think about how it makes you feel when you aren't present: are you panicked, stressed, stretched too thin? Then, how does being present make you feel? (Did you just take a deep breath like I did?)

Think of a task or project that consistently stresses you out. Think about how you could break it down into ten minute increments. You can do anything for ten minutes.

LET'S FLY

Chapter 17:

Thanks, Grief
(You're a Real B*tch)

I MAGINE YOUR CLOSE friend has a milestone birthday approaching. You conspire with her boyfriend, family, and friends to pull off an incredible surprise birthday getaway. Weeks of planning and preparation go into the event. Endless texts. Throwing her off the scent. Planning the most personalized birthday getaway and pulling it off to perfection.

It's all going smoothly... until it's not.

While in a dimly-lit bar amidst happy people dancing and toasting glasses of wine and rounds of shots, you feel that all--too-familiar inkling of sadness creeping up. Before you know it, it's taking over and you're quietly pushing tears away from your cheeks. You are praying everyone is at a good level of a vodka soda haze to not notice your tears and grimace. You hope the music is so loud that no one will hear your voice catch. No matter how hard you smile and plaster a look of "I'm having a great time," all you want is for the night to end so you can go back to the hotel, stifle your screams into a pillow, and cry yourself to sleep. And you don't know why. Nothing has happened to set you off. Everything around you is fun and happy. And yet, you feel like everyone is staring at you with a head tilt of pity or avoiding you like some sad widow plague, trying to harsh their buzz.

Now imagine this happening often, in all different types of ways.

This is grief. And she's a real bitch.

She rears her ugly head at the most inopportune times, and when she is least expected. In fact, the absolute toughest days for me are the ones I don't see coming. Of course all the firsts were heart-breaking: birthdays, anniversaries, Christmas, Mother's Day, Father's Day, Valentine's, New Year's Eve, etc. Those are awful. But, they often come and go with a quiet ease because I have prepared for them.

For me, the toughest moments since Jeremy died have been the ones I don't see coming. The first to catch me off guard was Thomas' last day of Kindergarten. Jeremy died on June 9 and I stopped going to Thomas' school. People noticed I wasn't around; apparently, some parents tried to get information out of teachers or my mum, who graciously did the pick-up and drop-off. I couldn't face them. But when I picked him up on his last day of Kindergarten, I felt the air go thick. My heart caught in my throat and I felt the tears brimming when I realized this was the first of countless milestones Jeremy would miss. The first thing Thomas would achieve without his dad.

My grief for Thomas' loss is heavy.

A boy needs a dad.

I was warned that grief affects people differently. For many months after Jer's death, other people's reactions and behaviour were the toughest things to deal with. It felt at times like I was being hit from all angles. Grief manifests itself in seemingly unexplainable ways. Psychiatric Social Worker Barbara Fane says you may find that your breath becomes short or shallow, appetite disappears or increases dramatically, and sleep disturbance or insomnia become an issue. Research shows that grief physically affects your brain. Grief comes at you in physical ways you don't see coming. Ugly, hurtful, irreparable ways. Grief is lonely, and when it needs company, it wakes me at 2 a.m. and keeps me up until 5. Sometimes it doesn't let me go back to sleep. It clouds my mind like an itchy blanket that I can't remove. It's like a fog combined with a dumbbell on my chest, always there, clouding all experiences. The tears are ready and waiting behind my eyes. Even in happy moments, sometimes it's impossible to crack a smile. Even when I'm not thinking about Jeremy or my current situation, it's there. Grief is always there. Relentless. A real b*tch.

In time, I have found the strength to gently move that itchy blanket. It's taken daily habits and working on myself (harder than I've ever worked on anything before) to build my cape after it was partially shredded by Jeremy's death.

A friend gave me an excerpt from Reddit that explains grief similar to waves of the ocean: sometimes overpowering and sometimes calm, sometimes you see the wave coming and other times it's blindsiding. This has been helpful and remains on my fridge. On the days grief is relentless and crashes over me, I have learned to lean into it and ride the wave. This too shall pass. MANY days it feels like it never will pass, but I have to believe it will.

Grief has been a b*tch, but also taught me so much. I can truly say that in grief, I have found myself. I have become so much more gentle and kind with myself. I've started listening to my inner voice and honouring her when she needs something. After losing Jeremy, I felt the need to make changes to my home, and one priority was my bedroom. It was the last place I saw Jeremy. It was where I found his suicide note. Countless people asked me why I wasn't selling my house immediately and how on Earth could I possibly even set foot inside the doors? But this was my home. Thomas' home. And it's where I feel the most calm. But that being said, changes needed to be made. My friend completely cleared out Jer's bathroom and helped me bag up his clothes. They sat in nine garbage bags in the storage room for a year before I did anything with them. We made the closet mine. I moved my bed and dressers and set up the space to be the calmest in the house. I kind of marvel that it's become my safe space. My zen den. This is thanks to grief.

Grief has taught me a lot. I set better boundaries. I am finally concentrating on what I want. Most of the time I realize I don't even know what I want but I am giving myself to space and time to figure that out. No longer quick to please others. No longer walking on eggshells. Grief has taken away a lot of my ability to entertain bullshit.

After we lost Jeremy, my mum recalls that I wasn't able to maintain a conversation or keep a thought for any amount of time. I don't remember this. I don't remember a lot of the first few months. I felt the air was constantly thick. Going through the motions of everyday life and parenting, while also being faced with the unimaginable new life as a widow. Therapy became instrumental in my grief, giving me the tools to just ride the waves and allow myself to feel the feels, as revolting as they were. I took my therapist's advice seriously and did the homework diligently, taking home notes to re-read when my fog lifted momentarily.

I am learning to judge myself less or at least catch it quicker. That night at the bar, celebrating my friend's birthday, I was so angry. I felt like a left-over: sad and standing out in a sea of two-stepping couples. I knew that I played a part in the dissolving of our marriage, but I was pissed at Jeremy for putting me in that booth, crying alone. My cape kept me company that night, and once I was back in the quiet of the hotel room, armed with my journal and pen, I realized that it was okay. I've learned that whatever I am feeling, that is okay. This has been huge for me. For years, I felt like I shouldn't feel how I did, and that my feelings were nowhere near as important as Jeremy's. Now I know I am important. Oddly enough, grief has taught me that.

I wouldn't do anything differently.

The cape has been with me through every step of grief. It quietly guided me through the hundreds of people at Jeremy's funeral. It was close behind me as I spoke with person after person following the service. It held my hand when I went back to work, three weeks later, still foggy but needing to keep my business afloat. It showed me that it was okay to feel the first glimpses of happiness and that it's possible to be happy while grieving, all at the same time. My cape reminded me that I was strong and resilient by quietly allowing any non-essential tasks to be bumped away.

We suffer grief not just in losing a loved one. We grieve the loss of a job, a divorce, an illness, a major disappointment, etc. Grief can come whenever life isn't turning out the way you thought it would. Our therapist even explained this to Jeremy and I. We were grieving the loss of what we thought being parents would be and what we had hoped for in Thomas' future.

Be kind to yourself in grief, no matter what stage. Whatever you're feeling is okay. It's important to feel those feelings and allow yourself to process what's happening. Rely on your cape to help you navigate what is important in your process and what isn't. Don't expect to know the answer to this right away. It's a process, but the cape will gently remind you of your strength and grit along the way.

Chapter 18

Take Action to Let Go

I REMEMBER TWO THINGS very vividly from one of our first dates. One, Jeremy remarking that he couldn't believe how open I was about my dad passing away three years prior. Two, me explaining my ultimate pet peeve: people who complain and never do anything to make a change.

Perhaps they did once my siblings and I went to bed, but I cannot remember my parents ever complaining about our circumstances. Not once did they play the victim, whine, or feel sorry for themselves. They were always positive, hard-working and goal-oriented, driven to create a beautiful life for our family. We weren't well-off, by any means, but I had no idea how much they struggled or how hard they worked to provide for us. My parents created a rich childhood, courageously moving us around the province of B.C. This mentality was cemented decades before I was born, when my dad emigrated from England at the age of 20. He sought a better future and knew he'd have it in Canada. His parents quickly followed with their two young daughters and my mum flew to join him with their wedding cake on her lap.

Talk about mindset. My dad always was the problem solver. He was a gentle soul with an enviable work ethic, which he inherited from my grandparents. I channel You Do You from Daisy McHale, my nana and my dad's mum, with pride. She embodied that mantra, always doing what was best for her family. She dove headfirst into any situation and figured it out. My nana met my grandad during World War 2, after he had lost his first wife and was raising his son alone. They quickly married, had my dad and then adopted two daughters. I don't believe Daisy ever met a challenge she couldn't conquer. Or a pastry she couldn't slay in the kitchen for that matter. My mum and dad learned from my grandparents and, in turn, they led by example, never playing the victim or complaining. They had goals and worked hard to achieve them, laughing at British comedies and listening to Queen along the way.

Because it wasn't part of our household growing up, I've always had an aversion to people who complain and don't get to work to improve their situation. Ever since I can remember, we gathered as a family to watch the six o'clock news. This was the beginning of me understanding that thousands of people around the world were suffering, and having the awareness that someone else has it much worse than me.

People often ask me how I've managed to continue on after losing Jer. Or after Thomas' two different special needs revelations. Or after losing my dad. My answer is always: I never felt like I had a choice. Of course I did have a choice. I could have packed it in. But I'm not wired that way. And I truly believe you can work to rewire your mindset, regardless of the hand you're dealt. In no way am I belittling your situation. Whatever hardships or issues you're facing, there is no doubt that they are huge. They seem insurmountable. You can't imagine how you'll ever see the light at the end of the tunnel. You can't imagine how it could get worse and then, oh wait, it does. You lose your job and your boyfriend in the same week you get the worst flu of your life. And then just to push you right over the edge, your washing machine leaks everywhere. And your landlord gives you notice.

We are all tested, and throughout life will face incredibly agonizing blows. To make matters worse, while you're down, it will seem like everyone else is getting promoted or engaged or hitting their goal weight. What gives? "Can I just catch a break?! Why does everything bad happen to me?!"

Alright, this where Tough Love Mare kicks in. (She's baaaaack!)

E-N-O-U-G-H. You want to improve your life? You want better outcomes? You want to be happy? Time to buckle down, stop complaining, and take action.

When you're complaining you are coming from a place of lack. The universe is always listening and always rooting for you, but you must send it the right messages. For example: "There are no good guys out there. All the decent ones are taken. I'm going to be single forever." The universe hears this as, "I don't think anyone is good enough for me, therefore, no one is." You may as well start looking at adopting a family of cats. Instead try this: "I am open and ready to meet the man who I am meant to be with. I know that I haven't come across him yet because I haven't been ready. I continue to work on myself and am ready when the universe deems it time. I believe he is out there working on himself too. I trust that good things are already mine." Yeah, it sounds hippy dippy, but if you want serious, real, joyful change, you're going to need to switch that mindset. And you're going to need to switch it every single time you catch yourself playing the victim.

Cue the cape. The cape is right behind you, waiting to give you strength to steer away from a complaint mindset or sense of lack. It's much easier to stay in bed, scrolling your phone thinking everyone has it much easier than you. But the cape is there to gently help you get up, put one foot in front of the other and start to make the shifts needed for a life of abundance, joy, calm, and whatever you want. Maybe it's a life filled with dancing in the kitchen while wearing fabulous outfits and going after your wildest dreams. You Do You.

Don't get me wrong. You do not have to be positive every hour of every day. Hell no. I'd be concerned if you were! It's okay to vent. In fact, it's imperative. Feel those feelings and allow them to flow through your body. But then, the work needs to begin. Showing that woe-is-me attitude the door and stepping into your power gives the cape the shivers. In a good way.

Let the Cape Help You Take Action:

Feel the Feelings: When something life-changingly awful and unexpected happens, more often than not we want to do anything but face those feelings. The idea of actually listening to our thoughts, our gut and our heart is the worst thing imaginable. It's no secret why humans gravitate towards a culture of numb, whether it's smoking, alcohol, drugs, food, a majorly over-scheduled calendar, mindless scrolling, over-exercise, or whatever your numbing agent of choice may be. Why would you want to get quiet? It sounds awful, because it is. Take it from someone who has been literally brought to her knees, body overtaken by emotion, screaming silently in disbelief and pain. But actually allowing yourself to feel the feelings is the only way to begin to heal and move forward. If you don't, I guarantee these emotions will manifest in awful ways. My previous doctor said he saw stress manifest physically all the time in his patients. That's the thing about emotions, they don't go away. They demand to be heard. So if you ignore, suppress, and numb those feelings, those emotions will rear their ugly heads in bad choices, physical illness, and a negative mindset.

Give Yourself Space: You're going to need to get distance to start to hear your inner voice. Your cape thrives on that inner voice and it needs space to know it's safe to come out and be heard. With that space, your inner voice will start to claw its way back to the surface. Mine was numbed for a few years and I always felt uncomfortable. The longer I left it, the worse things got. The one saving grace was writing in my journal. I needed to get quiet and sort out my incredibly confused feelings as I was struggling to support Jeremy in the last couple of years while caring for Thomas and keeping it all together. My friends were wonderful, but I got sick of re-hashing the same complaints. Sick of hearing my own voice. I also felt that it was time to lean on no one. I wanted to hear my own voice and find out what she wanted. So I brain dumped in my journal. Then another and another and another. I slowly felt an unraveling and, although there was no easy solution, it was comforting to visit my inner guide when I could. It gave me clarity with no outside influence. Driving is another way to give yourself space with no one around, just you and your thoughts. Getting out in nature is wonderful too, with no other sound but your breath and the fresh air. Sometimes even switching your physical space can make you see things in a new way. I love to rearrange a room and see what it unlocks.

Consider What You Want to Change: Brainstorm what's gotten you into this situation in the first place. This is the point in the Mareathon where you need to own your actions and *your* role in your situation. We do not waste time on blame. Only YOU are responsible for YOU. Harrowing things have happened to so many of us and I am in no way demeaning or negating their awfulness. But as Mareathoners, we do not dwell or blame. This solves nothing. In fact, it sets you back. You are the only person who is responsible to make the best of a situation.

Do Your Research: You do not need to reinvent the wheel. Talk to people. Tell people. You do not need to start from square one. Research. Ask people. Listen to podcasts. Read or listen to books. Watch YouTube. No one has been in your exact position, but you have so much to learn from their experiences.

Make a Plan with Executable Steps: I am a do-er. A checker--offer of to-do lists. Oh, how I love a list! I usually have at least three different lists on my phone and two in notebooks on any given day. While it's all well and good to have a list, you need a PLAN. Executable steps. For example: You may have "save money" on your big goals list. Well, that is so ambiguous I guarantee the cape will just scan over it, overwhelmed. What does that even mean?! I would make a list specifically for saving money and have things like:

- ★ treat myself to Starbucks on Monday only (take own mug for discount)
- ★ review subscriptions on Saturday to see which ones I can cancel
- ★ choose only one night of the week to eat out

- ★ meal plan
- ★ write grocery list
- ★ check flyers
- ★ download coupon app
- ★ grocery shop after lunch (never shop when hungry, trust me)
- ★ watch YouTube videos on saving money for inspiration and community
- ★ suggest a potluck games night next Thursday with friends instead of eating out

You get the idea. I'd add to that list of executable actions, your *why* you want to save money. Make something visual so every time you want to splurge, you come back to that reason and move on. Breaking your plan into executable steps makes it do-able instead of daunting.

Here's an example of how I created executable steps to achieve what seemed daunting and impossible: In the months after Jeremy died, I knew I wanted to change the house. It had been a scary place, riddled with anxiety, tears, and panic. Yes, there was laughter, love, and intimacy as well, but I wanted a real energy shift. And I wanted it yesterday. There was absolutely no way I was leaving my house the way it was. His death was palpable in every space, and everywhere I turned, I saw either a painful memory or a loving one that was just as painful. Some people judged me for making changes and were angry, but it was what I needed.

I wanted a calming energy on all three floors for Thomas and me, a space for us to feel safe to heal and to one day find joy. I wanted to unlock the front door and take a deep breath of safety every time I came home.

I made a list of what needed to be changed:

★ move my office from the laundry room basement to the second floor so I could see natural light while I sat at my desk (do this while family is here to help)

★ move the spare room to the basement (do this while family is here to help)

★ donate Jeremy's furniture to a local organization that employs adults with special needs (call and make an appointment)

★ rearrange my bedroom

★ clean out his closet and bathroom (leave clothes in storage room for the time being in case I want to keep any)

★ repaint the living room from bright orange to a calming grey (take your friend up on her offer to help with this while she's visiting in August)

★ paint the basement (hire someone for this big task, it's worth it)

★ buy and build new furniture for the basement television room (do this yourself to feel a sense of ownership)

★ add strings of twinkle lights in every room, for calming lighting

★ donate extra décor for a minimal vibe

I started two lists in my phone: one of things to do and one of things to buy. I slowly picked away at each. With every tick of a box, I felt myself moving towards peace and calm.

Get Going: This is where the cape really starts to flap in the wind. Once you have a plan, get to work. Make it as fun and enjoyable as possible. Don't look at taking action as a chore or one more thing you have to do. Listen, we all have more than enough obligations. This shouldn't be one of those—far from it! It should be something that's lighting you up, thawing your pain and easing your heart. It should feel like you are up-leveling and when you're not working on it you should be itching to get back to it. Remind yourself WHY you want to make these changes and WHY you are working so hard. I am consistently working towards a bright life for myself and for Thomas. I believe what we've been through is for a reason and I know why I work as hard as I do. Reminding myself why I am working hard and why I am changing is comforting, especially on the many days when I am so tired I can barely think straight. Once I had my list of house changes, I got to work. People were quick to offer help in the first month I was a widow. Even though I do not like to put people out, I accepted. Friends helped me with décor, purging, donating, painting, building, and moving furniture, etc. With every new item put in its place, and every paint brush stroke, I felt myself thawing. I felt proud to have a home for Thomas and I. Not only was I now the sole owner, paying the bills, but we had a safe and calm space. It felt like a major accomplishment.

Be Prepared to Pivot: The best laid plans and all. Yes, I am an advocate for the to-do list with an action plan. Yes, I want you to feel the feels, breathe, and take action. But I also want you to remember that life happens. When that ride takes you down an unexpected road and hits a pothole, it's okay. Be prepared to pivot. (And do it better than Ross does on *Friends*. You know I had to. "PIVOT PIVOT PIVAAAAAAAT!")

The cape will muster its courage and hold you as you pivot. You may feel yourself losing steam, feeling like you've pivoted so many times that you've done a full 360. Breathe. That cape has so much courage it will propel you in every turn. You can make a plan and take action, only to realize that your goals no longer suit you. You may get to a point in your execution where you reach peace sooner than expected. Just because you have a to-do list, doesn't mean you have to finish it. You Do You.

Self High Five: Don't get so set on your end goal that you forget to enjoy the ride. I see so many people miserable with their circumstances and believe that they'll never get out of their current rut, dead-end job or unfulfilling relationship. They are so miserable they don't give anything a chance to bring them joy. Celebrate the small victories! Smile and enjoy yourself along the way. It's not a sprint, remember. It's a Mareathon. And we are here to be present and enjoy each step along the way.

Every person is ultimately responsible for their own happiness.

You are not your circumstances.

You are someone who feels the feels, takes a beat to breathe, assess and then leaps into action with your cape while enjoying the ride.

You are not a victim. Again, as a Mareathoner, we've been through shit, but we don't act like shit.

Chapter 19:

Find Your Version of Healthy

W HEN I WAS thirteen my mum had a heart attack. I remember being annoyed with her that morning when she wouldn't drive me to school because she wasn't feeling well. I made a fuss then took the bus for another day of eighth grade. Instead of driving me to school, she drove herself to the nearest hospital. My seemingly normal day of school was interrupted when someone came up to me during a break in between classes to say that my dad had been pulled out of his class because my mum was in the hospital. What?! This was well before cell phones, so I had no way to get in contact with my family. The school secretary wouldn't tell me anything. When he came back to pull me out of school later that day, my dad said, "I always thought it would be me."

Then, six years later, it was.

My dad died instantly of a massive heart attack while laying on our couch watching TV. I'd already fallen asleep that night and woke up to my mum screaming on the phone to 911. We tried to revive him before the ambulance arrived. It initially drove right past our house and I remember having to run out on the gravel driveway, barefoot and braless in my pyjamas, to wave it down. They turned around and made their way into the house. He was laying on the couch, where he'd been watching the news before bed like every other night before. He couldn't be revived, so the paramedics hoisted him on a stretcher into the ambulance and raced to the hospital twenty minutes away. I drove my mum in our bright blue station wagon to the emergency room. My sister and her family arrived shortly after. We were told in a cold, fluorescent-lit room that he was gone.

He thought it would be him, and yet he couldn't be saved. Both my parents had heart attacks. One due to stress and one to obesity.

Do you think this was the beginning of my journey to being the healthiest I could be?

Nope. My reaction was to start smoking and consuming as much chemically laden, salty food as possible. I numbed myself with food, cigarettes, and sugary drinks. A couple years after my dad's death, I woke up with excruciating chest pains in the middle of the night, living alone, ten hours away from my mum. Do you think *this* was the beginning of my health journey?

Nope. I tried a path of attempting to eat salad (and more chips and French fries), yo-yo dieting and half-heartedly exercising for years. I legit would be on the treadmill *dreaming of the bag of chips and cigarette* waiting for me at home. Can you even imagine? I quit smoking. Then started again when Jeremy became suicidal. Then I quit again. Then I started up again the day he killed himself. I finally quit for good six months after his death. I used a free app that tracked how my health improved with every cigarette not smoked.

I needed to be healthy. I instantly became Thomas' only parent, which meant being strong enough to physically carry him if need be. I was the only one still around to care for him. I had to snap out of it, break the cycle and be the healthiest version of myself. If I wouldn't do it for me, I'd damn well better do it for my son. Both of my parents had suffered major heart attacks and I seemed on the path to follow suit. I vowed to change.

The year following Jeremy's death, I decided to go at my new year's resolution in a new way and instead to dedicate one word for my overall goals. I chose the word "health." I was ready to cut down my own walls and self-imposed roadblocks, to work towards being the healthiest I'd ever been. And then STAY there. This was the key.

Good health to me is all-encompassing. It's physical, social, and mental health. I wanted to have a healthier mindset, a healthier social life, a healthier relationship with social media. I wanted to find a way to love moving my body and a diet that made me feel energized and satiated. Healthy is relative and it should be what's best for YOU. What is your version of healthy? If you're nervous to start, don't worry, you're not alone. Most people are nervous and intimidated to take on a new habit. Start small and with one thing at a time. The cape will be there, right beside you, happy to get sweaty while you exercise or spice things up with a new recipe.

Things I've Incorporated in My Version of Healthy:

★ daily meditation

★ water with lemon before anything in the morning (this is good for digestion, your skin, hydration and a boost in Vitamin C to combat a cold or flu)

★ consistent water intake. An easy way to know how much water to drink is to take your body weight and drink half that amount in ounces (i.e. if you weigh 200 pounds, try to drink 100 oz a day)

★ taking reputable vitamins every day (this ensures I am getting the nutrients I need, helps with my energy, and boosts my immune system)

★ move my body as many times a week as I can

★ cap mindless social media scrolling

★ be intentional about who I follow online

★ limit alcohol

★ work daily on being present, grateful and calm—lots of deep, cleansing breaths throughout the day

★ mindful eating—but also allow for indulgences in moderation

★ gravitate toward positive, healthy people

★ loving self-talk

★ therapy

★ check in with family and friends regularly

I sought out people with the energy I wanted around; the people with similar goals and health aspirations. I cultivated the bedtime routine I'd always wanted. Baths, face masks, yoga, meditation, clean home, sleepy tea, delicious snacks, and a show to make me laugh. I loved that time between Thomas falling asleep and closing my own eyes: you have arrived at *Rejuvenation Station.*

My physical health is where I struggle the most. I've never been athletic or into sports. I rarely enjoyed working out and always felt incredibly inferior in any kind of physical activity. For example, I tried to work out at the gym. I found a lovely trainer who was encouraging and great at his job. I followed his plan haphazardly, but my gym time always took a backseat to my work hours. I'd have every intention to work out, but my desk would call and I'd get lost in the Mareathon. Before I knew it, Thomas was home and it would be yet *another* day feeling like a lazy failure. I decided to give classes a go. I figured this way I would be accountable and hopefully surround myself with like-minded, healthy people. I wasn't one of them yet, but I yearned to be. I couldn't even picture what it must be like to not have to wear shorts under every dress or skirt to combat chub rub. (For those of you who don't have to deal with this: *chub rub* is the oh-so-lovely feeling of having your thighs rub together so much so that the skin goes painfully raw in the summer. Neat-o, right?) I had always wanted to be one of the healthy gazelles who did spin at my gym. They, I assumed, had their health on point and in check. What I would give to be one of them. Terrified I would throw up or fall off, I signed up for my first class. Well, imagine how shocked I was when I survived! Not only did I survive, I wanted to go again. I felt safe in the darkness of the room, the beat of the music and the high-vibe atmosphere. It was like therapy mixed with a dance class.

I am still far from perfect with my health. I enjoy a glass of wine or a basket of fries as much as the next person. I miss days of meditation. I get sucked down negative social media rabbit holes. But here's a secret you need to remember and repeat to yourself: no one is perfect. Did you repeat it? *No one is perfect.*

Also, not one person has the exact same definition of personal health as the next. It's imperative to do some reflection and decide what good health means to you. Simply put, deciding what healthy means to you will then identify the small, daily, actions you take to shift yourself.

As you build a case for a healthier version of yourself, you will notice it build not only your physical strength and mental toughness, but also your cape will achieve gains. Taking care of your health in all forms from physical to mental to social will in turn add magnitude to your cape, strengthen its ties and allow it to lift a little lighter in the breeze. Every time you keep a promise to yourself by making your health a priority, you fluff out your cape a little more. Only you can take care of your health. Your cape is there to support you when it's tough, you're tired, or you just don't want to keep going.

Finding Your Cape:

Brainstorm what healthy means to you. Try not to include opinions of others in this description, or things like jeans sizes or a number on the scale. What is your version of healthy? Is it getting more sleep? Getting up earlier? Drinking more water? Eating out less? Setting a bedtime routine? Really think about how you could feel healthier, stronger, and more at ease.

I mentioned *Rejuvenation Station*. What would your station look like? Take a few minutes to close your eyes and picture the perfect thirty minutes before you fall asleep every night. What could you consistently do to ensure rejuvenation?

Chapter 20:

A Secret Antidote
to Bad Days

I'M GOING TO let you in on a little secret of mine. The best way to help yourself feel better on a bad day?

Well, you don't help yourself. You help someone else.

Honestly, this is another major shift moment. That cape is seriously going to puff out and propel you when you help other people. Let me explain.

My parents immigrated to Canada from England in their early twenties and then proceeded to work very hard, moving us all around the province of British Columbia. My dad became a high school mechanics teacher and, after a vacation in Canada's only desert, my parents decided that living in the Okanagan was their end goal. We lived in four different towns before I was ten and along the way my parents easily assimilated into each community, making friends and helping out in each town. They achieved their goal of living in the desert when I was ten, and we moved to a small, sunny, town. They bought what they hoped would be their forever home.

I remember one night, my dad got a call from a coworker whose car had broken down while he was in Alaska, and the first person he thought to call was my dad—because he helped everyone. My dad managed to talk his friend through car repairs long distance over the phone, so he wouldn't be stuck in the middle of nowhere. (I wish I could insert a round of applause.) He did that for everyone; he was always the first to offer a helping hand with a gentle spirit. My mum is the same, quick to help and offers to show up for people, even virtual strangers. She is a super positive person, too, easy-going and very calm.

That's the way it was when I was growing up: the understanding was that you give back. My brother and sister carry themselves in the same way, and are raising their kids accordingly. They'll happily give up their rooms when we visit, offer their toys to Thomas, and genuinely reach out.

You don't have to go over and above, but do something, say something, help in some way. It's always been ingrained in me. That's what I loved about radio. We have this platform to talk about community events. I wasn't necessarily donating financially to every cause, but I could give my radio time, my brand, post on socials, whatever. I loved being part of things, being able to help people, and it was a duty.

The National Institutes of Health reports that the MRIs of people who gave to various charities stimulates the reward centre in the brain, releasing endorphins. According to a study published in the International Journal of Psychophysiology, people who gave to others had lower blood pressure than those who didn't.

Back to the bad day. The next time you are having a bad day, maybe it's a rough time at work, PMS, a fight with someone, whatever. Do something nice for someone else. I find this to be the antidote to a bad mood.

Easy (and Inexpensive) Ways to Get Started:

- ★ let someone go ahead of you in line
- ★ smile at a stranger
- ★ compliment someone (without putting yourself down in the process)
- ★ buy one of the pre-made bags for the food bank at your grocery store
- ★ buy the person's coffee behind you in the drive-thru
- ★ donate clothes you no longer wear to a shelter
- ★ donate blankets you don't use to a shelter
- ★ pick a cause close to you and contact them to ask how you can volunteer
- ★ surprise a friend with flowers or a coffee
- ★ send a friendly, out-of-the-blue, text message
- ★ clear the snow off someone else's car
- ★ shovel the snow off a neighbour's driveway or sidewalk
- ★ share a fundraiser on Facebook
- ★ post a positive review for a local business

An effective way to snap out of a bad mood is to help someone else. As you can see, it doesn't have to be pricey, time-consuming, or involve a lot of planning.

I encourage you to add another layer to this. As you are doing a good deed, be present enough to realize how grateful you are to be able to be in a position to do this. Gratitude has the potential to overflow when giving to others. I'll use the example of paying for the person's coffee behind me in the drive-thru. I consciously think: *I am grateful that I have an extra few dollars to afford to do this. Grateful for the car I am driving. Grateful that my car keeps me safe. Grateful for my job to afford this coffee, this gas, and this car. Grateful to live in a safe country where grabbing a coffee is a no-brainer. Grateful for deep breaths and good music while I wait in line.* See? Generosity and gratitude go hand-in-hand. That bad day doesn't stand a chance! I don't mean "bad day" in a flippant way. These are all things that cumulatively helped immensely with grief.

Also, don't do it for attention or praise. Don't tell anyone you've done it. You need to do this for you and YOU need to self high-five. This is less about the person on the receiving end of the good deed and more about filling your own self-worth bucket. You can power up someone else's cape, giving it a boost, without them even knowing who did it. Once, I found out about a Mareathoner who needed help. She couldn't afford to get her eyes checked and needed new glasses. This meant she couldn't drive her son around because her prescription had changed so drastically. One of her friends messaged me, and I transferred her the money. I get lots of requests from people asking me to help with fundraisers. I don't say yes to everything, but I say yes to a lot. If I can't help financially, then I help with my voice and share it online.

You get what you give.

Karma, baby. The cape loves karma.

Chapter 21

Tribes Can't Be Forced

VER SINCE I can remember, my group of girlfriends has been everything to me. I have never been someone who has to be in a relationship. In high school I had crushes on boys, but besides a couple little flings (one that embarrassingly started and ended by passing a note... sorry Kyle!), I was always more than happy to be single. My girlfriends and I would spend hours listening to the Backstreet Boys, pining over Leonardo DiCaprio, seeing *Titanic* in the theatre 11 times, and making collages with images cut from magazines. I felt safe with my friends and utterly fulfilled. I soaked up the companionship of girlfriends and didn't need to date in high school. The thought of a serious relationship that would take time away from my friends just didn't appeal to me.

As I got older, things changed. I placed priority on my career, moving away for school and work. I've always been social, but radio can be a lonely industry, as the nature of the business can call people to move several times to advance their career. It's tough to maintain friendships when people are constantly moving. I moved too, and longed for that bond I'd felt in high school.

I was craving a close group of supportive, like-minded people who would push each other and be a cheering squad.

Always the one to take things into her own hands, I pitched the idea of "The Tribe" to seven women. I invited them all over one evening, and I laid it out, over drinks and snacks. We'd commit to hanging out once a month and become a tribe. Much to my excitement, they were all into it!

It lasted five months.

The plan was to meet monthly and we did have some fun times, initially. I got us all into a concert at a local nightclub and we danced the night away. We tried a spin class. We drank and chatted and got to know each other, but by the fifth month only three of us showed up. I officially let it go. To be honest, it hurt. I wondered why it was so tough to maintain adult friendships. I must have stunk up the room with my desperation.

In hindsight, this taught me that you can't force friendship. Reciprocity is a vital part of any relationship in my world. I want to get back what I put out there, but it can't always be that way. I tried so desperately to make the tribe work and my effort just wasn't enough. I do believe that the others wanted to be part of it, but life just got in the way and the timing wasn't right for a myriad of reasons. You can't force friendship and you shouldn't have to. It's wonderful when it can be organic and natural.

Your tribe will ebb and flow, pivoting with time and circumstances. In the wake of Jeremy's death, I actually lost friends who turned their backs on me, my grief too much for them to handle. One said to me that she didn't understand why I was still so sad and that she didn't recognize me anymore. She told me it was too hard and that I had changed too much. This was three months after his death. Just as Jeremy had lost friends when he went public with his mental health, I saw friends walk away from me after he was gone. I'd been warned this would happen, but nothing could prepare me for the absolute shock and pain it caused. I've learned that this is common in grief. On the upside though, I've made new friends in the last two years, ones who aren't turned off by my emotions. I find people who have experienced life and tough times of their own have really shown up for me.

As adults with responsibilities, we must be protective of our time. I seek out people who I feel good around. I want to be surrounded by people who are loyal, honest, loving, supportive, hard-working, happy, and striving to be better. Okay, they absolutely don't have to be all of these things all of the time, but you get the idea. Our capes are similar at times, fiercely propelling us to up-level and at other times, we ruffle each other's capes, as a reminder of our power.

Don't judge where your tribe emerges from. Let it happen naturally and surprise you. When my attempt at forcing a tribe failed, I created the Mareathoner Facebook Group. There's where I found my tribe. Naturally. Lovingly. Surprisingly. I had started to notice a camaraderie growing in the comments under my YouTube videos and thought it would be wonderful for a group of like-minded people to have a safe space online. It's become a real community where people share victories, struggles, ask questions, and some have become friends with each other offline, too.

I am often the person to reach out to make plans with my friends. Sometimes this gets under my skin and hurts my feelings. I've had stretches of time in my life when I've experimented to see if anyone would invite me out if I stopped making an effort. Even talked ad nauseam with my therapist about it. She made a great point to me one day that helped relieve this expectation and pressure: it's okay to be that person, because it yields the end result I desire. I want to see my friends and so I make plans to see them. Why waste time lamenting about how it happens?

Remember also that every friend serves a different role. Not all have to be able to chat with you about every aspect of your life and on every level. Some can be your fun friends, your work-out buddies, your keep-it-light gals, or the ones you share your most intimate secrets with.

I also want you to be very protective of yourself when it comes to friendships. Find the balance of being there for someone, without enabling their negative behaviour or compromising your integrity. You are a beautiful human being as you are and there are people who would be honoured to be your friend. In distancing yourself from a toxic friend you are in turn, being a friend to yourself. Just like social media, be aware of how you feel when you are around certain friends. If you start to notice that your anxiety spikes when you see a text come in, or you leave a coffee date feeling relieved that it's over, take note. This is your cape trying to tell you something.

Give yourself permission to realize that friendships have seasons where you can be more present or more distant. Also, you have permission to realize that friendships can wrap up naturally. Life ebbs and flows, and friendships will follow suit.

Our capes are filled with wonderful memories of feeling loved and supported by friends throughout different phases of our lives. Look for friends who will fix your cape and, in turn, make sure you keep an eye on theirs.

Finding Your Cape:

★ Think about what makes a good friend and what's important to you (and what's not).

★ Ask yourself what you are looking for in a friend and then keep an eye out for people who fit that mould.

★ Brainstorm what characteristics these people would have in their own lives (friendship aside).

★ Invest in what brings you joy, whether it's hobbies, exercise or entertainment. Chances are you'll find your people doing things you love.

★ Continue to work on yourself—be the person you'd want to be friends with.

★ Show up for your friends—checking in and showing an interest in their lives, even making notes in your calendar to remind yourself.

★ Make an effort to keep in touch and make plans. Everyone is busy—this is not an excuse.

★ Don't force it, but continue to be encouraged.

★ Don't put pressure on it; friendship is supposed to bring you JOY!

★ Remember it's about quality and not quantity. You'd be blessed to have a few close friends, rather than lots of acquaintances.

Chapter 22:

Ease the Cape's Load of Expectations

N OW, HERE IS something that will erode your cape: expectations.

Quite often, when you have expectations, you set yourself up for disappointment. You're already going into a situation, hoping it doesn't come up short, with a pessimistic attitude. Even if you have low expectations, it's still a negative mindset.

How do I know this? Because I used to let expectations rule and ruin my life.

I mistook expectations for standards. My excuse was just that I have high standards. Two very different things. Expectations are a belief that something will happen. Standards are a level of quality. In mixing up the two, I was believing that others would understand—without me telling them—the level of quality I expected and act accordingly. I assumed they knew what I wanted, so I was let down or disappointed. I started to realize the startling number of times I caught myself assuming. I now catch myself in my thoughts and am able to stop the expectations.

You may be reading this thinking, "Expectations keep

others in check, Mare." Or, "How am I supposed to have standards without expectations?" Yes, this can be confusing until you do some self-exploration and honestly ask yourself a simple question: What purpose does my expectation serve?

Here's the key: you can only control your *reaction* to circumstances and other people's behaviour.

For example, if your expectation is that someone is going to understand your point of view on a certain topic, why do you need them to agree? Will it reassure you? Give you confidence? Make you feel better about that topic? Following this rationale, you can see that it has nothing to do with the other person and actually is a bit selfish on your part.

My first big shift in managing expectations came when we prepared to lay Jeremy to rest. His funeral was a week after his death in June, but likely because of overwhelm, we decided to wait until September to spread his ashes. Side note: 10/10 do not recommend this. It was like reopening an unimaginable wound, as if we were learning of his death all over again. Some family could not travel back for the burial, so there were only a few of us there that day. I could not believe I was going back to the funeral home to, yet again, make excruciating decisions about his final resting place. Don't get me wrong, this particular funeral home bent over backwards to be accommodating and respectful. But returning to the building pierced my heart all over again. At the last minute, it was requested that we bury his ashes instead of scattering them. This meant long meetings and painful decisions. To design a headstone and choose a box for his ashes, trying to do what was best for everyone involved.

We were to bury him on a Saturday in September. As the day neared, my therapist and I plotted out how I would best endure the experience. She reminded me that the only thing to worry about was my own well-being and the well-being of Thomas. Full stop. That was my only job that day. I couldn't control how others would behave and it was not my role to comfort anyone else. This physically lifted a weight in my body. I'd been worried about how unimaginable this would be for everyone involved, but ultimately their grief was theirs.

I learned that weekend, and in the months to follow, that it's best to have no expectations about how people will handle their emotions. We can all agree to heal in our own way. Laying Jeremy to rest ripped me wide open. I remember collapsing at his grave, overcome with the finality of it all. But, because I had gone in with no expectations, I was a bit relieved by the end of the night. I felt some closure and, honestly, personal growth. I was proud of prioritizing myself and Thomas in our healing.

Practise catching yourself in what you expect. It's going to take courage, over and over again. And then again. That cape will hold you, silently cheering you on. Also, the weight of expectation is heavy, ease the load the cape is carrying.

Ways to Ease Your Expectations:

Ask Yourself Why: Take a mindful look at why you are creating these expectations. Often it's a way to protect ourselves from hurt or even prepare for someone to be hurtful, before they even have the chance. Where is this expectation coming from? If you were to take a moment, you would realize that this is your own mindset setting up these walls.

Adjust Your Self-Talk: You control your thoughts. Adjust them. For example, if your inner mean girl is rearing her ugly head, telling you that you look awful, show her the door. You are not defined by your looks. Hear me? *You are not defined by your looks.* Just as you are not defined by how much you do in a day or by how much money you make. You are defined by your character, how you treat others, and your footprint on this world. If you are feeling less than, remind yourself of a few reasons why you seriously rock. I personally have to do this out loud so I actually hear myself. Take a breather and listen to a good song. This is what it looks like to work on your self love.

Figure Out How to Get the Results You Want: If you are going in with the expectation that a meeting is going to be terrible, chances are it's going to be terrible. But if you go in determined to be present, polished, and positive, and do your best, then you're setting yourself up for a better chance. Yes, the meeting may still go sideways. Maybe you were hoping that giving your notice would make your boss offer a raise and beg you to stay. And then it doesn't happen. Well, you are now positive that leaving this position is what's best for you and your future. You did your best and that's all you can ask of yourself or anyone else.

Analyze Hurtful Relationships: If someone is consistently letting you down or hurting you, take a good look at this relationship. How does it enhance your life? Or, does it? Do you need this person in your life? If it's someone you see often, like a family member, and they always say something hurtful, why is that? Are they harbouring hurt from you from years ago? Is it years-old hate that can be addressed and healed? No? Okay, then how can you manage your behaviour to get through the interaction without being as affected? Be prepared that it's coming and know how you will react. My motto is "*Hurt people hurt people*." You can only control how *you* react, so have a game plan. For example, I struggle around low-vibe, negative people. I have to mentally and emotionally prepare to not be brought down. I go in with a plan, limit interactions and plan something uplifting after I see them. I highly recommend a positive playlist that can be busted out, at high volume, in the car afterwards.

Be Kind to Yourself: The last thing I want you to do is to judge yourself for having expectations. Expectations are completely normal, but it's important to manage them to garner the best result. Don't beat yourself up when you catch yourself in an expectation spiral. Just gently picture yourself turning a quick corner, to face the sun.

The more you can train your mindset to focus on you, your reactions and your behaviour, the more free you will be. This also pertains to dealing with other people's expectations of you.

People will forever have expectations of others. It's how we are wired. It's up to you to decide whether to accept their expectations as healthy and helpful or... not. And that's okay. In fact, that is some strong self-care and self-worth right there. Can you hear the cape is ready for take-off?

Here's a twist to show you how having expectations can be positive, likely because it leans more to the standard side of things. My expectation is that the people in my life are supportive of me and my grief. They show up, love me as I heal, and are ready to step in if I am behaving out of my values. Those who proved they weren't as supportive as I had expected, are painfully no longer in my life. I expect those in my inner circle to be accepting of Thomas and love him as he is. If not, you don't get the privilege of being in our life. Simple as that. Standards vs expectations.

Here's the bottom line: if you have expectations of others that aren't positive or healthy, you're opening yourself up to receive the same in return. Expectations are basically you saying how you want someone else to act. It can become a heavy weight on your chest when, ultimately, you have no say in the outcome.

The cape reminds us to be present and mindful of our thoughts. We control our thoughts and actions. You choose how you act and the cape attaches with courage to help you along the way. No one said this was going to be easy. But trust me, it's worth it and with the courageous release of expectations, your possibilities are endless.

Chapter 23:

You Are Worthy

B Y NOW YOU'RE getting that the cape symbolizes the voice in your head, your inner compass. The cape cannot function at its optimal level without its hem brimming with self-worth.

Self-worth is something to be nurtured, not taken for granted, and should be protected fiercely. Luckily, we've got a cape for that.

I had never considered self-worth until I got to a point where I needed to. I always figured I was confident, and that meant I felt worthy, right?

Confidence and self-worth are two very different things. I often wonder where my confidence comes from. Of course I have had bouts of questioning myself or low confidence, but in general, I have been confident as long as I can remember. I've always looked up to strong influences in current events, pop culture, and history.

Confidence does not equal self-worth. In fact, misplaced confidence is often a reflection of low self-worth.

Self-worth is loving yourself like you would a best friend. Knowing when to put up boundaries, when to say no, when to say yes, and respecting yourself to take a moment to con- sider what YOU actually want, need, and deserve. These are things that I had completely stopped doing. It made my skin crawl. It made me cry every day. It made me question every-thing. But I had no idea my self-worth was eroding.

Soon after Jeremy died, I physically collapsed with the rea-lization that my self-worth had slowly worn down to nothing without me even realizing it. This happened over time. I can't even pinpoint when it actually began to be sucked away like a low powered vacuum. But in hindsight, every time something awful happened or I made a decision I knew compromised myself, there went a piece of my self-worth.

I lost my self-respect, little by little, likely as I put Thomas and Jeremy first. I didn't know what else to do. And I do not for one second regret it. I had to put Thomas' complicated needs first from the moment he was born. Then, as Jeremy's mental health began to rapidly worsen, I helped him. This left very little for myself. That energy was spent on working and keeping the house together. The self-care was minimal and kept me afloat. A face mask here, painting my nails once in a while, going for a walk randomly, etc.

I stopped believing I was worth being put on the list of priorities in our family.

Self-esteem is minimized every time you concede or de-cide to make someone else happy or comfortable, even though it makes YOU feel worse. You brush it off, time and time again.

I grew up in a home where we were praised for being qui-et. Quiet at the dinner table while the nightly news was on. Years of therapy have made me realize this gave me the im-pression that I was not to speak up. (Ironic as I now talk for a living and am writing thousands of words in this book, no?)

I have been diligently working on my self-confidence since becoming a widow. I mindfully decided to strengthen my cape in the months that followed his death. I could feel the courage tightly up my back, propelling me to continue on in this new reality. The cape was hanging on, but could admittedly use some mending and nurturing. I consciously decided to not even consider dating for more than a year. I wanted to meet *myself*, figure out what I liked, wanted, needed, etc. I did not want to put myself in a situation where history repeated itself. Slowly, the cape was patched as I regained my self-worth.

If you are reading this and noticing your own cape could use some love by way of repairing your self-respect, here are a few of the things that helped me. Remember, this is an inside job.

Meditation: I know I have mentioned meditating earlier in this book, but the effects have been profoundly life-changing for me. It is impossible to think that you can hear your inner voice and what YOU want, with so much outside noise. At some point, the constant hum of the world needs to cease if you're ever going to find out who YOU are and what YOU want. It's only in the quiet moments, with no distractions, that your inner voice can be heard to say "do this," or "walk away from this," or "be careful around this person," etc. When the noise of everyday life is constantly screaming, your inner voice is stifled. She's trying like hell to be heard and to fight above the noise, but is constantly pushed aside.

Worthiness means listening to yourself.

No More Apologizing: There are many times I get uncomfortable when I follow my self-worth. For example, on a dating app a man revealed to me that he didn't have a job and that he'd lost his licence in a DUI. I said, very nicely, that we were not a match and wished him good luck. He shot back shaming me, saying I judged him too quickly and that maybe I should care more about getting to know him than his DUI. For a second I thought, "Am I being too judgemental?" (You're laughing, right?) Obviously not, but setting boundaries and knowing what I want in a new relationship seemed to constantly be a test of growing my self-esteem.

People pleasers take note: an enormous aspect of rebuilding my value has been figuring out what is important to me and not apologizing for it. A friend once told me she was sad to see how much I apologize for things that I shouldn't be sorry for. Talk about a wake-up call! She strapped on her cape to be straight with me and it has stuck in my head for years. I catch myself still and stop short of apologizing for something that I don't need to or, in fact, don't want to. This coming from a reformed people pleaser.

Worthiness means knowing when to apologize and when not to.

Time: Self-worth is a balance of putting myself first while respecting others and making space for their needs as well. I have also quietly been more mindful of who I spend my time with and also what events I say yes to. Sometimes I will feel the inevitable wave of guilt when I choose to say no, but that passes. If you go against your gut and say yes to something you don't want to do, you'll resent it. Stop being busy to avoid yourself. Learn to be okay in your own company. Remember that every time you say yes to something, check in to make sure you aren't saying no to yourself.

Worthiness means protecting your time.

Reciprocity: I value reciprocal relationships and I am choosing to place importance on this value. I have stepped back from relationships to see if the other person will make an effort without me doing all the work. Some have and others have not. And this is okay. Look for those who are cheering you on, supporting you, and lifting you up. Be mindful of people who want to steamroll you and gravitate towards those who feel like sunshine.

Worthiness means surrounding yourself with people who want what's best for you.

Oxygen Mask: I don't regret putting Jeremy and Thomas first. Not for a second. But I now know that it was not my place to drain myself and think that would save Jer's life. It wasn't my job to save Jeremy. In depleting my worthiness I didn't help anyone. Cue the oxygen mask analogy. If a plane loses cabin pressure, you must put on your own mask before you can help anyone else.

Worthiness means putting your oxygen mask on first.

Health: Focus on physical health, mental health, social health, online health, etc. Choose to no longer just be tired, but actually do the work to get better sleep. To have closer and more meaningful friendships. To not settle when dating. To exercise. To not drink alcohol just because you think you should. To take trips. To buy tickets to concerts. To not tolerate disrespect. Realize your value and then actually do the work to see it change you.

Worthiness means valuing your health, on all levels.

Quiet: Become more comfortable with quiet or silence in conversation. I used to be quick to fill the quiet to make someone else feel comfortable. I would say things I didn't really mean, just to put them at ease. Now, I am okay to let things hang in the air. When someone says something questionable, I pause. Let it hang. I no longer feel that it is my responsibility to make everyone else feel at ease at my own expense.

Worthiness is knowing that it is not your job to make everyone comfortable.

In the past, I often lived to make others happy and secure. Now I am doing that for myself. As I rebuild my worthiness one day at a time, I stand tall in knowing I did all I could, with my cape rippling behind me. I turn my attention and energy to Thomas with a newfound balance. I take care of me and I take care of him. My oxygen mask is firmly secured and you know what? Thomas is thriving! He's grown leaps and bounds in his development, all while I am valuing myself and my growth too. We are a team, taking care of each other with joy, love, and worthiness.

Finding a deep love for yourself takes the pressure off other people to fill that hole. If you are struggling, it's deeply rooted. These feelings are not your fault, but, if you don't do anything to work on it and build it back up, then it is your fault.

No one can do this for you and you better not look to anyone else to do it for you.

Get quiet and listen to your gut.

Worthiness means loving yourself like a best friend. Because you are.

Chapter 24:

You've Got This

WHEN FACED WITH making big choices, we are often jaded, not by our own fears, but by worrying way too much about what others will think. Chances are, they are so wrapped up in their own lives that they won't care.

Those who love you want what's best for you and will be supportive.

Indecisiveness often stems from past pain. If we've been hurt, we are less likely to want to put ourselves in that situation again. Survival instincts, right? But if we avoid something because it has hurt us in the past, will we ever grow from it? By no means am I suggesting that you continue to put yourself in a toxic or negative position. Hell no. Run with that cape billowing behind you. But, if you were hurt in a relationship, workplace, or friendship, does that mean that you don't deserve a healthy, positive one? Of course not!

You deserve health.
You deserve happiness.
You deserve joy.
You deserve safety.
You deserve to be authentically you.
You deserve to belong.

You deserve to be an equal in a relationship.
You deserve to feel loved, without parameters.
You deserve to know you matter.

The momentum created by the billowing of your cape will blow fear away, rolling like a tumbleweed in the rearview. You now have the tools to build and nurture your cape. Imagine it to be whatever colour or pattern or texture you want. Its size and shape are up to you. Perhaps it makes a sound or faintly plays a theme song when need be. Perhaps it changes colour depending on your mood or the situation. The cape is lined with happy memories, resilience, love, success, strength, and whatever else you weave into its patchwork.

My dad built a life-sized Superman that flew, despite the fact that it was heavy, not very aerodynamic, and had no landing gear. Despite everything it had against it, that Superman flew in front of countless people, always evoking the same reactions: awe and joy.

I want you to create a life that fires you up! I want you to create a life for yourself that elicits joy and makes you shake your head in awe at how wonderful it is. Your cape makes you as aerodynamic as possible, helping navigate through whatever forces come at you.

You are the one putting in the work, propelling yourself forward into a brighter future. You, the superhero with the cape, are saving yourself. You are not alone. Your cape can also wrap around you in a gentle hug, representing the people who love you, the Mareathoner community, and your own self-worth. A cozy embrace carried with you at all times. You're not alone and your cheering squad can't wait to see the greatness your cape and you do.

Now put on that cape and go do some shit.
Remember, you can do anything for ten minutes.
You've got this, baby. Listen to that cape as you fly.

Works Cited

Why Keeping a Daily Journal Could Change Your Life, Benjamin Hardy (LinkedIn):
https://www.linkedin.com/pulse/why-keeping-daily-journal-could-change-your-life-benjamin-hardy-2c

The Health Benefits of Strong Relationships (Harvard Health Publishing: Harvard Medical School):
https://www.health.harvard.edu/newsletter_article/the-health-benefits-of-strong-relationships

Go Easy on Yourself (New York Times):
https://well.blogs.nytimes.com/2011/02/28/go-easy-on-yourself-a-new-wave-of-research-urges/

How Vulnerability Can Make Our Lives Better, Brene Brown (Forbes Magazine):
https://www.forbes.com/sites/danschawbel/2013/04/21/brene-brown-how-vulnerability-can-make-our-lives-better/

How Do Thoughts and Emotions Affect Health (University of Minnesota):
https://www.takingcharge.csh.umn.edu/how-do-thoughts-and-emotions-affect-health

Science Says Healthy Scheduling Habits Make People Happier (Entrepreneur): https://www.entrepreneur.com/article/333169

Toxic Emotions Can Lead to Serious Health Problems (Huffington Post):
https://www.huffpost.com/entry/emotional-wellness_b_4612392

11 Intriguing Reasons to Give Talk Therapy a Try (Forbes):
https://www.forbes.com/sites/alicegwalton/2014/06/03/11-intriguing-reasons-to-give-talk-therapy-a-try/

Physical Activity Reduces Stress (ADAA):
https://adaa.org/understanding-anxiety/related-illnesses/other-related-conditions/stress/physical-activity-reduces-st

The Benefits of Meditation (Headspace):
https://www.headspace.com/science/meditation-benefits

Meditation in Depth (NCCIH):
https://nccih.nih.gov/health/meditation/overview.htm

Grief Symptoms: How Grief Affects the Brain:
https://barbarafane.com/grief-symptoms-how-grief-affects-the-brain/

Wanna Give? This is Your Brain on a Helper's High (Cleveland Clinic):
https://health.clevelandclinic.org/why-giving-is-good-for-your-health/

In Gratitude

My Editor, Simone Blais—You changed my life when you emailed, "I feel like your story could inspire so many others, and that's energy I would love to see in the world." Thank you for going there with me over and over again. I know that this was an overwhelming beast of a project at times and I am so grateful for your guidance. Thank you for elevating this book beyond my expectations.

Thomas—I love you. Thank you for teaching me so many lessons, giving me patience and so much love I am sure my heart will burst! I am a different person because of you and the role of being your mum is my greatest honour.

My Family—Whether you call me the Littlest Blister, Shrimp, Brat, Auntie Mari, Gorgeous, or Sweetheart, I am grateful for you. Thank you for showing me love without parameters.

Jeremy's Family—Thank you for the love you continue to show Thomas and for the grace you've given me in this journey. Thank you for sharing Jeremy with me and with the world.

My Friends—Thank you for being my tribe, both past and present. You are my sounding boards, give the best hugs, hold space for me to be upset, make a strong cup of coffee, and accept me for who I am as I ebb and flow with life. Thank you for the wine, the warm blankets, road trips, and hours of conversation. I'm the lucky one.

Janice—You said, "This will all be fodder for your book one day," and you were right. Thank you for being a mentor to me for more than a decade. You've always taught me to push past my self-limiting beliefs and led by example.

Sandra Richardson—You instilled a love of writing, reading, poetry, and Shakespeare in me in high school and I've held on to it since. Thank you for setting the bar high and for showing me at such a young age that anything is possible.

Vickie and Robyn—I cannot imagine the devastating state I'd be in without your guidance. Thank you for showing compassion and giving me the life skills and confidence to go to battle these past few years. In helping me, you've helped thousands, as I pass your lessons on. Thank you for turning me toward the sun.

Chelsea, Vanessa, and my Pure spin babes—Progress over perfection. Thank you for creating a safe space for me to work through my grief and push myself further than I ever imagined. Much of this book was worked out while on the bike.

The many women who care for Thomas and have created an incredible network of love for my son. Thank you for being my lifeline these past few years. I don't know where I'd be without you. This single mum is eternally grateful.

Meatball—I wish you were here to see your legacy. Perhaps you are. Thank you for loving me and for fighting for as long as you did. One half of Team Unstoppable continues on.

My Mareathoners—Life's not a sprint, it's a Mareathon. Thank you. You've changed my life, you've lifted me up, you've carried me through my darkest days, and been there to celebrate the joy. Thank you for being my tribe. My life is wonderful beyond imagination thanks to you. I love you.